A FRAGILE LIFE

A FRAGILE LIFE

Accepting Our Vulnerability

TODD MAY

THE UNIVERSITY OF CHICAGO PRESS   *Chicago and London*

The University of Chicago Press, Chicago 60637

The University of Chicago Press, Ltd., London

© 2017 by The University of Chicago

Published 2017.

Printed in the United States of America

26 25 24 23 22 21 20 19 18 17   1 2 3 4 5

ISBN-13: 978-0-226-43995-2 (cloth)

ISBN-13: 978-0-226-44001-9 (e-book)

DOI: 10.7208/chicago/9780226440019.001.0001

Library of Congress Cataloging-in-Publication Data

Names: May, Todd, 1955– author.

Title: A fragile life : accepting our vulnerability / Todd May.

Description: Chicago : The University of Chicago Press, 2017. |
Includes bibliographical references and index.

Identifiers: LCCN 2016022667 | ISBN 9780226439952 (cloth : alk. paper) |
ISBN 9780226440019 (e-book)

Subjects: LCSH: Vulnerability (Personality trait)

Classification: LCC BF698.35.V85 M39 2017 | DDC 128/.4—dc23

LC record available at https://lccn.loc.gov/2016022667

♾ This paper meets the requirements of
ANSI/NISO Z39.48-1992 (Permanence of Paper).

CONTENTS

PREFACE

I have been thinking about the central issues in this book on and off over the past forty-five years. For reasons that will become clear after the first few paragraphs, I have long been tempted by approaches to life that offer serenity, a still space that cannot be shaken. The views considered in the third chapter of the book and beyond—Buddhism, Taoism, Stoicism, to some extent Epicureanism, and the more recent work by Eckhart Tolle—promise that serenity.

And yet.

I have never been quite comfortable with that promise. In ways that I find difficult to describe, it has always sounded a false note to me. Of the two people in my life whom, at various times, I have felt to be wise, one called himself a Buddhist and the other, a Taoist. Their lives, while more at peace than mine, never seemed to conform to the image presented by what might be called the official doctrines of these views. I came to think that what I want, and perhaps what most of us want, is not what is on offer in those official doctrines. Not that they have nothing to teach us—in the final chapter I try to integrate aspects of their perspectives into my own view—

but rather that, at least in their official form, they envision a life that most of us would reject. They counsel invulnerability; what I believe most of us want, including many who hew to these doctrines, is a slightly less lacerating vulnerability.

This book is an attempt to work out how we might think about this vulnerability.

I would like to thank my colleague Yanming An for his help in navigating through some of the thickets in classic Buddhist philosophy. Needless to say, any remaining errors of interpretation are my own. My wife, Kathleen, patiently read the entire text and offered helpful suggestions. Audiences at the Copenhagen Business School, the New School for Social Research, and Clemson University participated in discussions of earlier drafts of several chapters. Those who cannot claim Elizabeth Branch Dyson as an editor should be jealous of those of us who can. She read the entire manuscript, and her comments on nearly every page vastly improved it. Two anonymous readers offered useful advice for revisions of the manuscript. Jenni Fry's copyediting protected the English language from my onslaughts. And, although this refers to my previous book, a thanks should go to Ryo Yamaguchi for his wonderful promotion of that book.

Finally, I would like to acknowledge Hattie Fletcher and *Creative Nonfiction* for permission to reprint a few pages of my article "Teaching Death," which appeared in their pages in 2010.

This book is dedicated to Kathleen, David, Rachel, and Joel. Cognizant, if not obsessed, with the fragility of all our lives, I persist in hoping for their flourishing.

OUR LIVES AND OUR VULNERABILITY

There are periods of my life when darkness threatens to envelop me. The image I have is that of a Queen of Darkness: powerful, inescapable, shrouded and shrouding. The Queen grips my shoulder. Sometimes it is more than that. Sometimes it is a full, cold embrace. I wish her arrival could somehow be announced ahead of time. There might be a signal, a warning, a note dropped off at my door, or a quick email: "The Queen is on her way." But there isn't. I never even feel the grip itself, the way one does when a friend touches one's back or a flirtatious acquaintance brushes one's forearm with a hand. The cold grip is there, the embrace is wrapped around me, the world is leeched of its brighter hues, all before I recognize what has happened. Nothing has turned to the good, nor will it ever. Or, if it has, that was all in the past. Before me there is left only to soldier on.

I get depressed.

Of course, that is not how I live it: I get depressed. That is not how anybody with periods of depression lives it. The depression is not in here; it is out there. And it is out there not as depression. It is not that others are depressed or that the world is depressed. Rather, it is that the world is structured poorly. It is badly put together. When I was younger, this poor structuring seemed more personal. Things were arranged so that my own life wouldn't work out. I was living a meaningless, mechanical existence, like everyone else. However, I among them had the misfortune to know this, and not only to know it but to feel its meaninglessness deeply. On the subway I would see the empty faces of my fellow riders and wonder how they could not recognize the poverty of their own lives, a poverty that was etched into their features. The old Chinese woman with overfull shopping bags staring straight ahead; the construction worker slumped and asleep after a day too tiring to allow him to enjoy his evening; the businessman holding a *New York Times* in the classic folded position, looking like every other businessman holding the *Times* in the classic folded position. It was all so pointless. How did they not see it? And why was it given to me to be tortured by that recognition?

I am older now and realize even in my worse moments that the world is not arrayed against me. And so, when the Queen of Darkness decides to visit, there is no conspiracy against me. The futility is equally distributed. We are all born to no point, live out our days as best we can, and are then dissolved into the earth. It is not just me, and my recognition of this is not a peculiar form of torture. My wife will live in disappointment for having married someone who could not meet her expectations, reasonable though they were. My children will suffer in ways I fear I can foresee but am helpless to prevent. The misery and disappointment and despair and loss and pain that are the lot of so many lives become salient to me, they crowd me, dimming the light of the world until it is difficult to see anything but their shadows.

It is not that, at these times, I cannot go on. There are those, I know, who cannot. The weight of the Queen upon them presses them down into their beds, or stuffs them into a bottle of whiskey, or renders them incommunicado. A friend of mine, who does not call it the Queen of Darkness but the Pit of Doom, finds herself in one or another of those places when she is in the Pit. It is not like that for me. Fortunately, I can keep going. In fact, over the years I have learned to hide our acquaintanceship. Recently, I mentioned to a friend over lunch that I was in such a period, and he commented that I didn't seem any different from how I usually am. So, no, it is not so bad for me as it is for many. And at this moment, as I write, when the Queen is not near—or at least does not *feel* near—I know that in the end I am lucky. There are much worse depressions that people suffer, and other, worse things that people suffer than periodic bouts of depression. And, more important, I know that my life has many good fortunes, only a few of which I might deserve. On the scale of human suffering, I'm a lightweight.

And yet the Queen does visit me, and then the world darkens. I can deal with it. I do deal with it. But the visits do not cease. I do not recognize their coming; they slip into my days unnoticed. In fact, I often do not recognize the darkness as anything other than the world's truth until the embrace is loosened and the hues brighten again. (I did recognize it at that lunch recently, but the visit had been going on a while by then and the worst had passed.) That's why a notice, some advance warning, would be helpful. But, of course, that's not how it works.

What should I make of this? How should I integrate these visits into my life? How can I think about or take up my life, given that I have these visits, without just thinking of them as periods to be endured? Or maybe that is precisely how I should take them up. Maybe there is nothing else to be done except undergo them alongside the other sufferings that life necessarily throws up before us.

I have a friend whose early life seemed charmed. When she was younger she was a model and a film producer. She came from a family that was very rich. Her one child, a son, was socially conscientious; he worked distributing humanitarian aid in poor countries. It was a life many of us could only dream of. Then her son was killed in an accident in the course of his work. Since his death, she has taken up the mantle of humanitarian aid and has done an extraordinary job of it. Her work is a daily reminder of her son's life, but also of his death.

We all face suffering of one sort or another. Our lives are disrupted; seemingly insuperable obstacles rise up before us; we become bereft of someone we love or someone we need. How do we deal with this? Or, since dealing with it is often a matter of coping at the moment, how can we think about ourselves and our place in the world that will allow us to go on the best way possible? We will see, in this chapter, some of the myriad sources through which most of us are vulnerable to suffering: physical, psychological, moral. And we will see, in the following chapter, two sources of vulnerability that none of us, lucky though we might be, can escape. How do we cope with the vulnerability of our lives, if not simply by facing each crisis as it comes and hoping it all gets better? Is there some way of conceiving a larger picture of our place in the world in which these sufferings, whether or not they can be justified or even make sense, can at least be accorded a place that brings us solace if not peace?

As we will see, there are at least two ways such a picture might be drawn. I have given these two ways names, unlovely ones to be sure. Their unlovely character is even more jarring in that at least one of these pictures—the one I will ultimately reject—strikes me as quite beautiful. This picture, which is common to a number of doctrines, I will call *invulnerabilism*, and the contrasting one, which seems to me the right one for most of us, I will call *vulnerabilism*. I do this with some hesitation. Throughout my philosophical career, I have tried to avoid jargon. It seems to me that philosophical writing is often rife with needless obscurity. To be sure, there are times when technical vocabulary of some sort or another is required to make a point. Philosophy can be difficult. However, I believe that the excuse of technical or conceptual necessity is overblown in my field. There are many important things that have been said in philosophy that, if stated with more clarity, would provide interesting food for thought to a wider audience.

In my own commitment to avoid jargon, I have, among my personal maxims, this one: do not make up new words without serious justification. And here, at the very outset, I have coined not one but two new words. My justification for doing so—and only the rest of the book will tell whether this justification is adequate—is that the distinction I am drawing will be easier to bear in mind if I use these labels. It is not that this distinction has not been recognized before. I am surely not the first to draw it. However, the distinction so shapes what is to come that it is handy to have terms, even these homely ones, to mark it. I promise the linguistic coinage will end here.

Invulnerabilism can be associated with such doctrines as Buddhism and Taoism from the East and Stoicism and perhaps Epicureanism from the West. Vulnerabilism, however, is not entirely divorced from these doctrines. It recognizes their insights and seeks to draw on them. Ultimately, though, it will reject a central tenet common to all of these views, or at least all of them in what I will call their official form. Vulnerabilism rejects the idea that we can make ourselves invulnerable to the world's predations. Thus the two names.

We will, as we progress, need to sharpen the idea of invulnerability and with it the idea of vulnerability. Invulnerabilism is not the idea that the world cannot make us suffer at all. After all, if I stub my toe, it will hurt, and no doctrine, however tenaciously embraced, can prevent my feeling the pain of a stubbed toe. But invulnerabilism is not, or at least not primarily, about stubbed toes. It is about how we can relate to our lives such that many of the things that normally make us suffer will not do so. As one of its consequences, it will give a place to stubbed toes such that, although they might hurt, they will hurt less than they would if, say, we thought of our stubbed toes as examples of how life is ultimately pitted against us. But that is a minor consequence of a larger picture of how to take up our lives.

According to the invulnerabilist, we can—and according to many, we should—develop a place of peace in ourselves, a place of detachment that ultimately cannot be touched or shaken. This becomes our core. It is the development of this core which makes us ultimately invulnerable to the misfortunes that befall us. It allows us to secrete a certain distance between us and what happens to us such that, although we might be affected to a certain degree (invulnerabilist views differ on this point), we remain unmoved at the core of our being. We are like spectators of a sentimental movie or fans at a basketball game: we may feel the sadness or excitement of the moment but know that, in the end, it is only a movie, only a game. As the contemporary spiritual writer Eckhart Tolle says, "the more you are able to honor and accept the Now, the more you are free of pain, of suffering."[1] We will discuss invulnerabilist views more specifically and in more depth in chapter 3, but what they all have in common—what makes them all *invulnerabilist*—is their commitment to the importance of rendering ourselves immune to what preys upon us.

By contrast, the vulnerabilist view I will develop here rejects the idea that we can or should develop such a core. It does not deny the importance of coming to some sort of peace with the world, although perhaps the better term would be *truce* rather than *peace*. It embraces some of the insights of invulnerabilist views, insights that allow us to avoid becoming abject before our suffering. Moreover, vulnerabilism can allow that, for some, invulnerabilism might work as a way to live. However, for most of us, not only would we be unable to develop an invulnerable core; we would not want to. Although we might take up aspects of invulnerabilist doctrines, or exercises associated with them, we seek to do so not to secrete a distance between ourselves and what happens to us but instead to be able to handle it a little better. Vulnerabilism concedes—indeed embraces—the idea that we can be shaken to our very foundations. What vulnerabilism looks like begins to become clear near the end of chapter 4 and is more fully developed in the final chapter.

*

In order to approach the issue of vulnerability, we will need to canvass different types of vulnerability. But before that, we must confront a prior question. What is a human life like such that it can be vulnerable to suffering in the first place? What makes us capable of anguish at what happens to us? Humans and some other animals are susceptible to sufferings of which many living beings are not. Mice can feel physical pain, but they cannot, like chimpanzees or humans, feel embarrassed. Nor can they feel disappointed—at least they cannot feel disappointed in the failure of a long-term commitment, since mice do not have any long-term commitments. And chimpanzees, for all their genetic proximity to us, cannot feel disappointed in the outcome of a presidential election or the ending of a novel. Although all living beings with a decent neurological apparatus can suffer physically, humans can suffer emotionally in ways that are barred to beings with less developed—or even alternatively developed—brains.

It is not merely the existence of our particular type of brain that matters, though. It is the way we live, a way that requires our type of brain but is not explained simply by pointing to the tops of our heads. To ask about suffering, then, or about the suffering we humans are exposed to, leads us to the prior and more general question of how we live. In philosophy, things are often like this. The process of answering certain questions leads to other, more basic ones. And here at the outset we already encounter this. Understanding how we can suffer requires that we first understand how we live.

We humans live primarily through what we, following the philosopher Bernard Williams, might call *projects*, to which we are committed with deeper or shallower engagement.[2] A project is a set or group of activities that unfold over time, usually (but not always) in a progressive order. We do projects, we are involved in projects, and we shape our lives through the projects we are involved in.

To see this, let's look quickly at a few examples and then linger over a couple of others. Eating a good meal at a restaurant is not a project, but learning to be a chef is. Watching a sporting event on television is not a project, but coaching is—and it may involve, as one of its activities, watching game tape or a sporting event on television. Jumping into the water to cool off on a hot summer's day is not a project, but developing oneself as a swimmer is.

What projects have in common is that they unfold over time. Moreover, they often evolve over the time that they are unfolding. Coaches develop their knowledge of the game, their ability to see what is going on in their sport, and their capacity to assess the skills of their players. Swimmers become more conversant with the water; they articulate their bodies in a more efficient fashion. Chefs learn what spices go with what ingredients and can eventually expand their repertoire to incorporate different spices and ingredients in new combinations.

But it isn't just these types of activities, which are just hobbies for most of us, that are projects in this sense. Friendship and love relationships are also projects. They are in general more important ones, what Williams calls "ground projects" or what I will often call *central projects*. Williams notes that "a man may have, for a lot of his life or even just for some part of it, a *ground* project or set of projects which are closely related to his existence and which to a significant degree give a meaning to his life."[3] These projects engage us at a deeper level than our hobbies do. They are woven into our sense of who we are and what we are about. The loss of a close friendship or a love relationship is experienced as a loss of some part of oneself. And what goes for these relationships also goes for a good career or a long-term engagement with a social justice movement or involvement with a church. It can go for something like a commitment to youth sports, in which case coaching becomes more than a hobby and instead part of who the person is. In all of these cases, our sense of self is tied up with our projects. We should think of these kinds of projects as more than just discrete sets of activities or engagements that we happen to find ourselves doing. Of course there are those kinds of projects as well, but central projects are more significant, bound up with who we are and the sense of meaningfulness our lives have.

In order to see this, imagine someone without any projects: no engaging career, no close relationships, nothing she is involved with that seems important, and no hobbies. It becomes hard to get a grip on a person like that. It is not just the point of living this way that becomes difficult to grasp; without any projects, the very substance of her being seems elusive. There seems nothing—or at least very little—there. When I try to imagine this for myself, I sense large parts of myself evaporating, leaving behind either a thin mist or at most an anonymity that could be anyone but in which I don't particularly recognize myself.

We might ask here whether almost everything we do is tied to a project in one way or another. It would seem so from the description I've given. But what would we say of a situation, not an uncommon one, in which someone is involved in a job that is not so much a career but rather a rote repetition of tasks? This could be someone working on a mind-numbing assembly line or in a fast-food restaurant. It could be a lawyer who finds herself faced with cases that begin to look the same after a while or a middle manager shuffling papers that seem to have no connection to a product worth producing. People in these positions are certainly involved in their work for a large part of the day, nearly half their waking hours. However, let's assume that they are not engaged by their work. They find it alienating. Rather than being mentally challenged or fulfilled by what they do, they instead turn off their minds as best they can from the time they clock in until the end of the workday. It is something that they do solely in order to make money, and for no other reason.

Are these kinds of jobs projects? Or do projects, in the sense we're speaking of here, require emotional or intellectual involvement? On the one hand, these jobs are sets of activities that one does over time, even if there is no progressive development associated with them. On the other hand, people who do these jobs don't see them as part of themselves. These jobs don't contribute to a sense of who they are. (There may be offshoots of such jobs that do contribute to that sense, though, such as the development of a community of friends.) Furthermore, some people only do certain of these jobs, for example fast-food service, for a short time, say as a summer job or as a way to make money between more fulfilling positions. (One of my sons spent the latter years of high school making the rounds of fast-food joints. We would occasionally spend an evening discussing the various merits—both culinary and vocational—of McDonald's, KFC, and Burger King.)

In the case of short-term jobs, like summer jobs, I don't think we would be tempted to call them projects. However, if someone is working a particular fast-food job or in a factory-type law office or a large, impersonal corporation over the course of many months or years, it does begin to assume the status of a project. This is not because she identifies with it in the sense of being emotionally connected to it. Often people don't. Instead, it becomes a project because, even if it does not concern a person's *sense* of who they are, it does concern *who* they are, or at least who they become through long-term involvement. Jobs like these can become alienating projects; they are projects that, precisely because they require so much time and often give so little in return, contribute to a sense of one's life as being something one would like to escape. To be sure, such projects are not central projects. One's central projects are what one does outside of these jobs. But they are projects nevertheless.

This should not be taken to mean that service jobs of these types must necessarily be alienating. They might not be, although their character makes alienation difficult to avoid. It could be, for instance, that a particular fast-food restaurant has little turnover among a staff that is enjoyable to be around, that particular tasks are rotated so that nobody is stuck doing the same thing all day, and that it is attended by a regular set of friendly customers. In a case like that, we can imagine someone who feels engaged by the work and who draws a sense of themselves from it. Given how such jobs are set up, this would be an exceptional case. But it is not beyond imagining.

The projects I'm interested in here are not the alienating involvements but rather the significant ones, the ones that are important *to us* in our sense of who we are. They are the projects that not only give definition to us but are also the ones we want to give definition, the projects through which we seek to express and characterize ourselves. These are not always the ground projects Williams refers to. The net I'm casting is a little wider than that. But they are projects that are important to how we conceive ourselves and what we want our lives to look like.

But if humans are the type of animal largely constituted by projects, how do we adopt them? How do we come to take up some projects as ours and leave others to the side? Here I can only gesture at an issue that I have taken up elsewhere at greater length.[4] Our projects are embedded in nets of social practices. We don't simply make up our projects from thin air. Each of our lives is woven into the lives of others, institutions, and places. This is true even for those who largely live alone. It is not simply the personal interactions with others that help form who we are—although that is important for most of us. At a deeper level, the unfolding of our lives is in debt to the history of practices to which we have been subject.

To see this, let's first understand what a practice is. In an earlier book I offered a technical definition of a practice as "a regularity (or regularities) of behavior, usually goal-directed, that is socially normatively governed."[5] What I meant is this: A practice has certain regular ways of acting. Those ways of acting are guided by explicit rules or implicit norms regarding how a person goes about things in that practice. Moreover, those rules and those norms are not made up by individuals; they are part of the social fabric. Baseball, for example, is a practice. So is child rearing. Psychotherapy is a practice, or perhaps a group of closely related practices. Every profession has its practices, as do hobbies and other activities like church going and bird watching. Even solitary activities like writing a diary are practices. What makes all of these things practices is that there are ways of doing them that people recognize, rules and norms that characterize what is and what is not a participation in those practices. Somebody who stands on the church steps singing a Beatles song may be engaged in some sort of practice, but if so it is certainly not the practice of church going.

The rules and norms of a practice are not static, and often they are not very restrictive. Practices evolve and change, and with them, the rules and norms of that practice. This can happen in many different ways. Sometimes the rules or norms of a practice—the proper ways of going about it—are challenged. In painting, for instance, the norm that painting should represent something in exterior reality was challenged over the course of the late nineteenth and early twentieth centuries. This led to a new conception of what the practice of painting was about. At other times, the rules or norms may be challenged by what is happening in the activity. When the great basketball player Wilt Chamberlain starting playing professionally, several rules had to be changed in order to accommodate his talent, such as the rule about how close a player could stand to the basket for more than three seconds. Without those rule changes, it would have been impossible to engage in a fair game against him. In psychotherapy, there are often challenges to how it is performed, which lead to changes in a practice or perhaps even new practices of psychotherapy, as recently with the emergence of what is called narrative therapy. In contrast to traditional psychotherapy, narrative therapy does not see people's problems as coming just from inside them; it recognizes that people's problems are often a product of their environment. Moreover, there can be disputes about the proper way to engage in a practice, disputes that are difficult to resolve. Think here of the various disputes that have characterized the history of religion, such as changes to the liturgy of the Catholic Church.

Alongside the dynamic character of practices is the fact that many of them, while defined by rules and norms, allow for a wide variety of activities that conform to those rules and norms. Chess allows for a variety of strategies, as do different sports. Psychotherapy involves different interventions with different people as well as the development of the discipline through new learning, all within a general set of norms of psychotherapeutic practice. University pedagogy, in which I'm involved, admits of different teaching methods, from lecture to group discussion to (my usual approach) Socratic questioning. More recently, it has incorporated—at least for some,

I don't count myself among them—new technologies that have been used in different ways. So we should not think of practices, although they are governed by rules and norms, to be static and monolithic. Instead, practices are dynamic and evolving on the one hand and, at least usually, open to many different types of activity on the other.

With this background, we can begin to see how people adopt particular projects as their own. Everyone is raised in and exposed to a variety of practices. These practices differ across cultures and even within cultures. At the very earliest stages, there are child-rearing practices to which we all are subject. But soon enough other practices come into play. For most children, various schooling and sports practices begin to assume a central importance alongside practices that involve the building of friendships. However, even at this stage we can see differences among cultures developing. For instance, in my current residence of South Carolina, church going is a practice into which children are inculcated at an early age. For most children here, it is at church along with school where peer friendships develop. This contrasts with New York City, where I grew up. For many children there, churches (or synagogues or mosques, which are few and far between in South Carolina) don't play as central a role in social life. I did not attend religious services during my childhood. This was not considered unusual. In the part of South Carolina where I reside, my children found it difficult to develop social networks without aligning themselves with a church.

A deeper and more disturbing difference in exposure to practices happens to many women, who in various countries are prohibited from participating in a number of public practices. This prohibition impoverishes them in several ways. First, it denies them access to developing the skills associated with those practices. Think here of the prohibition against women driving in Saudi Arabia. Second, it denies them the social interaction associated with those practices. Third, and most relevant for us, it denies them access to activities that they might adopt as projects in their lives. If one is not allowed to access to the public realm, one cannot become—at least not without great difficulty—a politician or a university professor or an athlete.

This leads us to the heart of the matter regarding practices and projects. It is through our exposure to and participation in practices that we become molded into the people we are, develop the values we hold, are drawn to the activities we participate in, and ultimately choose the projects we engage in. Those who are exposed to practices of painting or sculpture might choose them as projects, whereas those who are not aware of their existence or are prohibited from participating in them cannot. It is in and through the practices with which we come in contact that we choose the projects—or, sometimes, find ourselves involved in the projects—through which we largely define who we are.

In saying this we should not forget that those projects, inasmuch as they are practices, are dynamic and changing and commonly internally open within their norms. So choosing a project is not like choosing an item on a menu, where you get that particular item fixed that particular way. Rather, a project is a way (or several ways) of acting and being with others. One can not only create oneself through the practices one chooses as one's projects; one can modify the practices themselves and in certain cases one can change them fundamentally. Gandhi and Martin Luther King Jr., for instance, through their rigorous insistence on nonviolence, changed the character of political resistance by opening new avenues of action. It might be said that they created new practices of resistance, although this would not be entirely true; there were practices of nonviolent resistance that preceded them. However, through their rigorous conception of and engagement with nonviolent protest, they articulated a new set of norms for protest that allowed for new ways of participating in resistance to oppression.

It may sound here as though projects are nothing more than a subset of practices, that subset that people choose to adopt as their own. That would be misleading. Projects of sculpturing, church involvement, writing novels, engineering are all practices or sets of practices. One might wonder whether the same goes for friendship. Friendship is a project in the sense I've been talking about here. But is it a practice? It certainly involves practices—there are ways of expressing and developing friendship that have their own norms and even a few rules, and these norms and rules vary by culture. But in asking whether friendship is a practice, the concern might be different. Even if friendship involves these norms and practices, one doesn't engage in friendship *as a project* in the same way one engages in, say, sculpture as a project. And one certainly doesn't seek to follow norms of friendship in the same way one follows, say, the rules of chess. Friendship arises out of and expresses personal warmth or love. What place do these emotions have in projects and, particularly, in practices?

The difference between friendship and sculpture or chess, however, is less significant than it may seem. It is true that in the latter cases the norms might be more explicit than in friendship or love relationships. However, we must bear two other things in mind. First, while implicit, norms of friendship do exist. There are norms about the kinds of activities that express a friendship and those that diminish it. Gift giving, discussing important topics, engaging in common pursuits are activities that are expressive of friendship. But if I tried to enhance a friendship, to show my caring for my friend, by sleeping with his girlfriend I would not, in our culture, be enhancing the friendship. Even if I genuinely felt that the reason for doing so would be to show my friend that he had good taste in girlfriends, I would still be violating a norm of friendship that would diminish the relationship between us.

Second, although other projects involve learning one's way around the norms of a practice more explicitly than is usually done in friendship, the point of their being projects has to do with one's caring about them. Someone may not love doing sculpture in a way she loves a friend. But to make sculpture a central project in her life does involve loving to do it, or, if the word *love* is to be reserved for interpersonal relationships, then it is a matter of caring a lot about doing it. Moreover, inasmuch as sculpturing becomes a central project, its rules and norms can become a sort of second nature. The artist no longer thinks about them but instead comes to embody them in her approach to sculpturing—sometimes literally embodying them in her hands. In that way, sculpturing as a project can become like friendship in the sense that a person is taken up in the flow of it such that the norms and rules that characterize it are no longer explicit. They form part of the background of a person's actions, unspoken and even unfelt, although, as with friendship, they are there nevertheless.

We might say, then, that projects, and particularly central projects, involve or are expressed through practices (or at least primarily through practices) but that they are more than simply engagements in those practices. Rather, they are significant, caring engagements in or with the objects of those practices. They are engagements that matter, engagements through which we largely identifies ourselves. This does not mean, of course, that our engagement is simply about ourselves. If I am engaged in sculpturing or friendship, it is largely because I care about sculpting or about my friend. And it does not mean that these engagements need to be morally worthwhile. A person can be engaged in projects of terrorism or undermining others or destroying a worthy community. However, it is through those engagements that my sense of myself, of what I am about, largely arises. We might say that my sense of who I am arises not so much when I look inward at myself as when I look outward at what I do or, more precisely, at what my projects are.

*

Our sense of our selves, then, is tied up with our projects, which in turn are inseparable from the practices in which we are immersed. With this sketch of how we live in hand, we are ready to confront the question of the ways we are exposed to suffering.

We can immediately recognize that many of the ways we are vulnerable to sufferings of various types will come from things that affect our ability to engage with our projects or in those practices in which our projects take place. This is not to say that we aren't vulnerable in other ways. But humans (and perhaps other cognitively advanced species such as dolphins, elephants, and the great apes) are exposed to a vulnerability that is often, although not always, a matter of disruption of our projects. We can consider in particular physical and psychological sources of vulnerability as well as conflicts between projects before turning to a source of vulnerability that is not solely a matter of projects, that of moral luck.

Vulnerability rooted in our physical nature is, of course, something we share with other animals. We are corporeal creatures, subject to injury and damage in our environment. Any animal that is in sufficient pain finds it difficult to focus on its daily tasks. At times that difficulty can turn into an impossibility. I once had a kidney stone—a sizable one, as I later found out. Apparently, there are three places in which the corridor from kidney to bladder narrows, and it is in those narrowings where all the pain happens. Although my stone never made it through the third narrow (it had to be surgically removed), I will never forget the pain of the first two. In both cases I wound up curled in a fetal position on the floor, the layers of my personhood stripped away. Essentially I became for those moments an agony surrounded by a body. I imagine the pain of childbirth is something like this, although, of course, I cannot be sure.

This does not distinguish the vulnerability that arises from my body from that of many other animals. (And of course often the suffering—equal in intensity and of longer duration—that nonhuman animals are subject to is of human origin.) We have in common with other animals a corporeal existence that renders us physically vulnerable. However, there are differences between human vulnerability to pain and that of other animals. The philosopher Jeff McMahan argues that pain in nonhuman animals may matter less to them than an equivalent pain for humans, for several reasons. First, for humans, "the badness of pain is not entirely intrinsic. Pain is also bad because of what economists would call its 'opportunity costs'—that is, because it excludes or prevents people from doing or experiencing things that would have positive value."[6] Nonhuman animals—at least most of them—don't suffer from the loss of other opportunities that they can conceive but not accomplish. Moreover, people can suffer from the anticipation of pain and from concerns about the medical significance of pain in ways that most nonhuman animals cannot. Finally, since human life is often longer, chronic pain may cause more suffering than it would for an animal that will live a shorter life.

On the other side of the ledger, however, humans might have compensating commitments that take their minds off the pain and thus lessen it. Involvements with a career or church or social justice movement can occupy someone's mind in a way that is not available to other animals. Their pain may more likely become the center of their world in a way that humans might avoid through having their minds engaged in other activities.

McMahan's view should be seen through the lens of humans as creatures of projects. The suffering we undergo with physical pain not only affects our ability to engage in our projects but also gives rise to anxiety about our ability to do so in the future. Because projects unfold over time and because humans have a sense of their future, physical pain can induce psychological suffering in the form of concern about our projects. The sculptor with carpal tunnel syndrome and the athlete with a torn ACL will not only experience pain but also be worried about what their injuries mean for their future participation in activities that have conferred meaning on their lives. Not all pain will do this. Deep physical pain—kidney stone level pain—blocks concern about projects because it blocks everything except the awareness of the pain itself. And at the other pole, mild discomfort affects our ability to engage in our projects only marginally and so is unlikely to be a source of worry.

On the other side, however, as McMahan points out, because humans are oriented toward the future, the suffering associated with physical pain might be blunted. If I can, while in pain, still do what is important to me, still write or paint or design a bridge or swim every day, then I have a solace that many animals do not. The relation of physical pain to one's projects, then, is double edged; it is capable of interfering with those projects and creating worry about the future ability to engage in them, while at the same time those projects might offer ways to staunch the effects of physical pain. Which edge is the more important depends on the nature and level of pain and on the projects in which one is involved.

Not all physical sources of vulnerability are rooted in pain. There are ways in which, depending on one's projects, physical limitations that are not painful, or at least not very painful, can interfere with the projects through which one identifies oneself. The documentary movie *Hoop Dreams* portrays two high school basketball players from Chicago with enough talent to make it at the collegiate level. One of them, William Gates, although a standout player, struggled with a knee injury that reduced the number of college scholarships he received. Eventually he was recruited by Marquette University, but his knee problems limited his playing time. He was to get his degree at Marquette; however, his project of playing basketball was often stymied by the physical limitations around his knee. For Gates, the problem was not one of physical pain. All basketball players deal with pain. Moreover, the impairment of his playing did not lie in physical suffering. Rather, it was that his body could not carry through on the central project he had set for himself.

The fact that a central project is stymied should not, by itself, mean that the life of the person whose project it is would itself be stymied. It is possible that, while a person's central project could be undermined through physical limitations, the person can be capable of developing other projects. That turned out to be the case with William Gates, who graduated Marquette with a degree in communications and went on to develop a career as a pastor. His dream of playing basketball did not leave him, however. He later tried out for the NBA but was again impeded by an injury, this one to his foot.

For others, an inability through physical limitation to engage in a central project can be more devastating. Luis Sharpe is a former football player who was an outstanding tackle for the professional football team the Cardinals, a team he joined when it was in St. Louis and then moved with it to Phoenix. He was selected three times to play in the Pro Bowl, the postseason game for the best players of the season. He was regarded as a team leader. He also had a drug problem, particularly with cocaine. During most of his thirteen seasons he was able to keep the problem under control, with the exception of a short period of rehab. However, in 1994 he tore a ligament in his left knee and never played again. It is unclear whether he could have returned to football, but he felt he would not be able to play at the same level he had achieved before, and so he quit the game.

After that, his life descended into crack cocaine and prison. He spent most of the next fifteen years in prison and was released in 2013.[7] A recent film on his life indicates that he is currently drug free and involved in volunteer projects in the local community.[8] Even if he maintains a drug-free existence, however, the effect of his losing a central project is manifest. Although he had drug problems during his football career, he was able to keep his life more or less on track as long as he played football. Once that project came out from under him, however, he lost himself for many years.

Our corporeal nature opens us to a variety of ways we can suffer. Many of us will find ourselves limited over the courses of our lives as our capacity for physical pain or limitation disrupts or even undermines projects in which we're engaged. For most of us, those projects are not central or ground projects. Perhaps we run to keep in shape, but then our knees or back becomes weak, so we switch to swimming or work out on an elliptical machine. Or we do yoga but develop a bad shoulder and so turn to jazzercise or t'ai chi. Having to change exercise routines or give up a hobby rarely creates a crisis in our sense of who we are or what we are about. For others, however, like Luis Sharpe, the fact a person is a corporeal being can, when that corporeality is exposed to injury, damage their lives in more profound ways.

Our physical nature is one source of our exposure to suffering. Another source lies in our heads. The complex psychological makeup of human beings (and, as always, certain other species) exposes us to a number of injuries, limitations, setbacks, obstacles, and frustrations to which a less cognitively complex being would not be subject. If we combine our psychological makeup with the related fact that we are creatures of projects, it is not difficult to recognize that there is a wide array of ways in which humans are psychologically vulnerable. Of course, the other side of this vulnerability is that there is also an array of joys and satisfactions that can attend a human life that are unavailable to those in many other species. A mouse, for instance, cannot know the pleasure of learning higher math or winning a campaign for racial justice. However, for our purposes it is the exposure to suffering to which our makeup subjects us that is at issue.

One way in which psychological vulnerability might manifest itself is through a tendency toward depression. This is what I described in the opening pages. In a sense, most depression is like physical pain rather than physical limitation. It makes it more difficult to engage in projects without undermining our ability to do so altogether. As I mentioned, when I am visited by the Queen of Darkness I can soldier on, often without it being recognized by those around me that She is currently residing in my life. There are others, however, who suffer severe depression and for whom the ability to function at all is compromised during their dark periods. For them, continuing to engage in any of their projects is too difficult. The weight of their depression pins them to their beds or numbs their minds to the point where any activity is beyond them.

If mild depression is like physical pain in that it does not undermine our ability to engage in our projects, it is unlike the physical limitations we saw in the cases of William Gates and Luis Sharpe. For them, the limitations were focused on particular central projects. Mild depression rarely inhibits a particular project. Rather, it suffuses a person's projects, spreading its shadow across all of them, making them seem more distant or unachievable or pointless. We should not think, however, that all physical limitations are restricted in the projects they disturb or that all psychological difficulties are diffuse across projects. People who are confined to wheelchairs or who have severe medical conditions are barred from participating in a number of projects. The physical limitations to which they are subject affect them not only with regard to specific project but more broadly in the way they navigate through the world. This does not mean, of course, that they cannot engage in projects at all. Consider, for instance, the remarkable career of Stephen Hawking, who suffers from amyotrophic lateral sclerosis (Lou Gehrig's disease) but has achieved stunning success as a theoretical physicist. However, what physical limitations such as these do entail is that, like depression and significant physical pain, suffering can spread across projects rather than remain confined to one.

On the other side of the coin, there can be psychological difficulties that are sources of suffering within specific projects rather than across them. A friend of mine, a remarkable philosopher, has done significant work in advanced logic, a field that requires a level of intelligence and concentration that is beyond me. He has told me that as he has gotten older his ability to concentrate has diminished to the point where it is difficult for him to sustain working on a problem for more than several hours at a time (which is nevertheless longer than I could focus at any point in my philosophical career). This decline does not affect his ability to engage in other forms of philosophical reflection which, for him at least, can be accomplished without the kind of focus that logic requires. (One hears similar stories in the areas of mathematics, chess, and physics, where the greatest accomplishments are often made by people in their twenties.) This limitation is not a source of deep concern to him, since it does not affect him in other areas. However, inasmuch as he would like to continue his accomplishments in advanced logic, it is a limitation that he wishes had not beset him. It is, then, a psychological difficulty that affects a specific project of his rather than spreading across them.

Before turning to the arena of morality, I should pause to address a concern that might have arisen for readers in the discussion of physical and psychological sources of suffering. You might ask whether the distinction I have drawn between physical and psychological sources of suffering is artificial or misleading. Aren't psychological phenomena also physical phenomena? After all, it is the deterioration of certain areas of the brain that has led to the decline in my friend's ability to concentrate for long periods. Moreover, there can be sources of suffering that would not easily be placed on either the physical or psychological side, since they would seem to involve both. Certain types of brain injury would fall into that category. This is a vexed issue in philosophy, one that, fortunately for me, is wide of our concerns here. My division into physical and psychological is not meant to imply that they are two different realms. Rather, it concerns our perceived sources of suffering. Some forms of suffering arise from what happens to what we perceive as our bodies as physical objects; other forms arise from what happens to what we perceive as our mental states.

To the question of whether physical suffering results in psychological suffering, the answer is, it depends. Severe physical suffering of any kind is likely to have psychological effects, as the examples of kidney stones and childbirth display. However, there are people who have, say, chronic low-level knee pain who do not find this debilitating when it comes to their lives. Perhaps someone is not an athlete but is instead involved in intellectual pursuits that don't require use of the knee. She has the ability to concentrate that is not undermined by mild pain and is not worried about what the pain signifies (she has confirmed that it is inconsequential to her overall health). In a case like this, although the pain is physical, and although we are physical beings even in our psychological makeup, it would be a stretch to say that physical suffering must lead to psychological suffering. The fact that psychological suffering is physical, then, need not entail that all physical suffering involves psychological suffering.

We have been looking at two different sources of vulnerability to suffering—one rooted in our corporeal existence and the other rooted in the complex nature of our psychological structure. In both of these cases, we have seen that suffering, in addition to being caused by pain itself, often emerges from the disruption or even undermining of central projects. There is a third source of vulnerability, one that stems from projects themselves and particularly from conflicts that may arise between them, conflicts that need not be under our control. Let us turn now to that third source.

In her essay "Morality and Partiality," the philosopher Susan Wolf makes the case that we ought to think of impartiality as a central aspect of morality. That is to say, morality ought to be a matter of taking everyone's interests equally seriously. This might seem to be an obvious point, but it's not. Consider parental relationships. Most of us would think it strange if a mother acted toward the interests of another's child with the same solicitude that she acted with toward her own. It is one thing to step back and recognize that neither child is worth more than the other in the larger scheme of things; however, it is quite another to act on that recognition. And there are moral philosophers who would argue that there is something *morally* wrong with, say, a father's treating another's child equally, something that goes beyond the psychological effects it might have on his own child or the fact that he is better placed to care for his own offspring.

Wolf denies this. In her view, partiality is not something to be incorporated into morality but instead involves a set of values that should stand alongside morality. Morality, in other words, ought to retain its impartiality but also ought to be seen as one among several sources of important values in human life. Whether this is so (and I believe she has offered a convincing argument that it is) will not concern us here, since the point she makes about conflict will be relevant for us whether or not morality should be considered impartial. However, one of the examples she offers, that of a conflict she sees as one between love and morality, speaks eloquently to the problem of potentially clashing projects. "Consider," she says, "the case of a woman whose son has committed a crime and who must decide whether to hide him from the police. He will suffer gravely should he be caught, but unless he is caught, another innocent man will be wrongly convicted for the crime and imprisoned."[9]

Wolf's argument is that we should see this example as one between the love the mother has for her son and the requirements of morality rather than as a moral conflict itself. (It also illustrates another source of suffering that we have not discussed: that associated with the *suffering of others* that one cares about.) If the mother decides to hide her son, she is, Wolf thinks, acting in a straightforwardly immoral manner, and we can recognize this while also admiring the woman for her commitment to her son. As she puts the point, "To describe the woman's conflict as one *between* morality and the bonds of love seems to me to capture or preserve the split, almost schizophrenic reaction I think we ought to have to her dilemma," and concludes that "*she* had reached a point where the issue of moral approval had ceased to be decisive."[10]

In order for the mother to reach this point, however, she had to be committed to both her son and morality. In other words, without both her son and morality being projects of hers, there would be no conflict. Moreover, without their being central projects, there would be no emotional dilemma. On the one side, if morality was not important to her, she would not have had to "reach a point where the issue of moral approval ceased to be decisive," because moral approval—whether her own or someone else's—would not have mattered in the first place. It is possible that she would have liked to have *appeared* to be a moral person, just because her dealings with others would be easier if they thought her so. But she would have had no real dilemma of her own. For her, the situation would simply have been one of how best to care for her child in a set of difficult circumstances.

On the other side, we need not go so far as to imagine that she didn't care for her child deeply. We can instead imagine the woman as one of those people who takes the idea of "law and order" so seriously that anyone who commits a crime needs to receive proper punishment. Her son would be no more above the law than anyone else, and for someone to act to shield him from proper punishment would be unaccept-able. In this case, her son could still be a project of hers, but he would not be a central project—or at least nearly as central as her morality.

The dilemma, then, arises from a conflict of central proj-ects. And once it arises it becomes a source of suffering, no dif-ferent in this way from the physical or psychological sources of suffering we have already seen. Moreover, like those two latter sources, its emergence is not something that just hap-pens to her, outside of anything she happens to do or believe. We might say that, as a result of her central projects, she find herself suffering. Because of this, there is a way in which she is the cause of her suffering. Had she not been committed to both of these projects, there would not have been suffering, or not nearly so much. Similarly, if athletes were not committed to projects that expose them to injury or my friend to ad-vanced logic, then injury or a loss of mental edge would not be a source of suffering. For many people, it is because of the role that projects play in our lives that we find ourselves suffering in ways that appear difficult or perhaps even impossible to avoid. Of course, as we have seen, not all suffering is directly rooted in projects: physical pain and psychological debilitation are sources of suffering that do not stem from commitments we have undertaken. However, among their deleterious effects are those that hinder us from adequate participation in those commitments, from projects we have undertaken and from which we derive our sense of who we are.

There is one other source of suffering we should consider here, one that does not stem from a conflict of our projects but rather from a general commitment to morality—that is, to being a morally decent person. Philosophers describe this problem as one of "moral luck." It might seem strange to think that one can be lucky or unlucky in a specifically moral sense. We will pause over that possibility in a bit. However, before turning there let us linger over the problem itself. There are two classic articles on moral luck, both aptly entitled "Moral Luck." The first is by Bernard Williams, whose work we have already seen with the concept of ground projects. We will take up his article in the following chapter in another context. The other one, written a few years later, is by Thomas Nagel.[11] Nagel offers us several types of moral luck to consider, but to grasp the problem in its immediacy, consider one of his examples, that of a truck driver who accidently runs over a child.

As Nagel points out, one can feel a sense of regret for having accidently hit a child even if one had no fault in the matter. Perhaps the child ran out into the street from between two parked cars, or was pushed by someone else. "However," Nagel considers, "if the driver was guilty of even a minor degree of negligence—failing to have his brakes checked recently, for example—then if that negligence contributes to the death of the child, he will not merely feel terrible. He will blame himself for the death. And what makes this an example of moral luck is that he would have to blame himself only slightly for the negligence itself if no situation arose which required him to brake suddenly and violently to avoid hitting the child. Yet the *negligence* is the same in both cases, and the driver has no control over whether a child will run into his path."[12]

The truck driver's ill fortune in killing the child exemplifies, for Nagel, the larger phenomenon of moral luck. "Where a significant aspect of what someone does depends on factors beyond his control, yet we continue to treat him in that respect as an object of moral judgment, it can be called moral luck."[13] He isolates four different kinds of such luck. First, there is constitutive luck, the luck of what kind of person we are. Someone who is naturally empathic with others is morally luckier than someone who is not, because they will more likely see the right thing to do in a wider array of circumstances. Then there is the luck of what kinds of situations a person finds herself in. Nagel points out that someone who grows up in Nazi Germany would be morally unlucky, since it would be harder to be a moral person under those conditions: more effort is required to be moral, and it would be more dangerous to be a morally good person. "Ordinary citizens of Nazi Germany had an opportunity to behave heroically by opposing the regime. They also had an opportunity to behave badly, and most of them are culpable for having failed this test. But it is a test to which the citizens of other countries were not subjected."[14]

Third, there is the kind of luck involved in the history of how someone comes to be the person he is. This is like constitutive luck, but it is a matter of environment rather than nature. Someone who is abused as a child or taught that other people's feelings don't matter is less likely to be morally sensitive than someone exposed to a more nurturing education or one that leads them to recognize others as worthy of moral consideration. Finally, there is luck in how things turn out. This is the luck faced by the truck driver. It is also the luck faced by those who undertake acts of rebellion for the sake of freedom from oppression. "If the American Revolution had been a bloody failure resulting in greater repression, then Jefferson, Franklin, and Washington would still have made a noble attempt, and might not even have regretted it on their way to the scaffold, but they would also have had to blame themselves for what they had helped to bring on their compatriots."[15]

For Nagel, the combination of these types of moral luck poses a threat to moral judgment. If our nature and our formation and the circumstances we find ourselves in and the outcome of what we do are all subject to luck, then it seems we have very little control over the space in which we can be morally judged. And without control, how can moral judgment take place? "The area of genuine agency, and therefore of legitimate moral judgment, seems to shrink under scrutiny to an extensionless point."[16] The issue for us is different. To the extent to which one seeks to be a moral person—that is, to the extent to which being moral is a central project—one can suffer as a result of moral failures over which one had no control. The truck driver who could not control whether a child would run out in front of his vehicle, the person living in Nazi Germany who was incapable of living heroically, the abused child who grows into a person who serially abuses others and then regrets it, or the person who joins a rebellion against an oppressive regime only to see the rebellion crushed and their family murdered when their identity is discovered: all of these people suffer because all of them seek to live a moral life.

A true sociopath—someone who had no consideration for

morality or no empathy with the lives of others—would not be exposed to this kind of suffering. For such a person, being moral is not a project. Most of us find such people repellent. We not only expect others to act with moral decency toward us, but we seek to be moral ourselves. It is an important element of who we think we are. We can see evidence of this in the reaction we often have when we're accused of a moral shortcoming, of being unfair to a subordinate or failing to see that our child is depressed. Our response is often one of justification. The problem, we say, is not that we were acting immorally, but that we were justified in our actions given the circumstances, or we were ignorant of some aspect of the situation we could not have reasonably known. But we are rarely capable of saying to ourselves, Yes, I was a moral failure at that moment.

If being moral is a central project for most of us and if Nagel is right in thinking that we can be morally unlucky then moral luck stands alongside our corporeal nature, our psychological structure, and the conflicts we face among our projects as another source of vulnerability to suffering. But suppose Nagel is wrong. Suppose moral behavior is actually under our control. The problem, one might say, is that Nagel has failed to see that moral behavior has nothing to do with circumstances. It is only a matter of our intention. A good moral act is defined as one that emerges from an intention to act rightly. And because we are in control of our intentions, there really is no such thing as moral luck.

In considering this possibility, the first thing to recognize is that embracing the idea that morality is solely a matter of intention would lead us to some odd moral conclusions. If morality lies in intention, then the truck driver with unchecked brakes who was lucky enough to avoid hitting a child because no child ran in front of his truck is just as morally guilty as the one who hit the child. He should regret his failure just as much as the unlucky driver. Moreover, on this view there is no moral distinction, even if there is a legal distinction, between murder and attempted murder. Both involve the same intention. The abused child who abuses would be cut no moral slack, because their intention would be no different from that of a well-raised child who went on to be abusive. And we would have to come to the same judgment of Washington, Franklin, and Jefferson if the American Revolution had failed rather than succeeded. Either they would have been responsible in both possibilities for exposing their compatriots and perhaps their families to a pointless death or they would have been responsible in neither case.

However, even if one accepts these judgments as consequences of one's moral view, the problem of moral luck would not be solved. The point of grounding morality in intention was to render morality under an individual's control and therefore deny that it could be a source of suffering. That is, I could always choose to be a moral person by having the right moral intention and so avoid the suffering associated with moral luck. However, even our intentions are not entirely under our control. They are responsive to circumstances that are beyond us. We might see this at a first go if we recall Nagel's discussion of constitutive moral luck and the luck of how we were raised. The kind of people we become is not entirely under our control. We are molded in ways that make us likely to have certain kinds of intentions rather than others. This raises a challenge to those who would seek to avoid moral luck by appealing to intentions. Even so, though, someone could insist that with a supreme effort at self-control and through habitual molding of himself, it is possible to overcome the tendencies of nature and the misfortunes of upbringing.

There is another difficulty, however, one that is not so amenable to such a solution. As Joel Feinberg, the late American philosopher of law, argued, we often do not have control over our intentions in much the same way that we cannot control the consequences of our action. In a famous example, he asks us to imagine a hemophiliac, Hemo, and someone who has slapped him, Hotspur. Before slapping Hemo, Hotspur had to form the intention to slap him. This intention need not be something he reflected on before deciding to swing. It could be that he felt insulted by Hemo and immediately formed the intention. Now, Feinberg asks us, "Imagine that we have photographed the whole episode and are now able to project the film in such very slow motion that we can observe every stage of Hotspur's action and (constructively) even the 'inner' anticipatory stages."[17]

At this point, we can stop the film and linger over each of the instants at which the intention to slap Hemo was being formed. But now, imagine another person, Witwood, who is exactly like Hotspur and finds himself in exactly the same situation. However, something happens at the moment Witwood is about to slap Hemo that prevents his anger from arising. "For example, at the stage when Hotspur would begin to burn with rage, a speck of dust throws Witwood into a sneezing fit, preventing rage from arising." Or "at the point when Hotspur would be right on the verge of forming his intention, Witwood is distracted just that instant by a loud noise. By the time the noise subsides, Witwood's blood is cooled, and he forms no intention to slap Hemo."[18]

In this case, Witwood's failure to form an intention that he would otherwise have formed is not entirely under his control. External circumstances intervened that prevented its arising. If we rewind the film slowly enough, we can imagine this intervention to have happened at any point, so that the entire sequence leading from the cause of Witwood's potential rage to the full existence of the intention to slap Hemo would be subject to circumstances that would prevent its emergence. Here we can recognize that not only are the consequences of our actions not entirely under our control: neither are our intentions.

To be sure, the example of Hotspur and Witwood is an unusual one. However, we need to grasp the full implications of the example. It is not only the existence of the dust or the noise that prevents Witwood's intention from arising; it is their nonexistence in Hotspur's case that allow the intention to arise. In other words, for most of our intentions to come to fruition, the world has to cooperate at the very least by noninterference. We are immersed in a world that sometimes allows our intentions to arise and sometimes frustrates them so that they never see the light of day. It was as much bad luck for Hotspur that nothing prevented his intention from forming as it was good luck for Witwood that something did.

We may, then, add moral luck to the physical, psychological, and conflictual sources of vulnerability to suffering that we saw earlier. When we do, we recognize that we live in a world where our capacity for suffering can come from many sources, very few of which we have much control over. Invulnerabilism, as we will see, recognizes how little control we have, and seeks to render us immune to suffering precisely on the basis of that recognition. It seeks, we might say, to abstract our being from the world in a specific way, not so that we are uninvolved in the world but so that that involvement does not lead to suffering. By contrast, the vulnerabilism we will see emerge in the final two chapters does not hope to prevent our suffering but rather to allow us to cope with it in a more satisfactory way than we otherwise might. Or at least it will allow us to cope with much of it. There are sufferings that are perhaps beyond our ability to cope with, and in some cases beyond our even wanting to cope with them.

However, before turning to the next chapter, let us pause just long enough to recognize an implication of the fact that the sources of vulnerability that lead to suffering are not, or largely not, under our control. As we have seen, we may be exposed to suffering without our being able to do anything to prevent it. However, because of our lack of control it may also be that we are *not* exposed to suffering through no credit to our own action. Just as we may be unlucky, so we may be lucky. It is possible that none of the sources of vulnerability we have discussed so far actually leads to suffering. Perhaps we remain healthy throughout our lives, both physically and psychologically, and can participate adequately in our projects and realize them in significant ways. Perhaps we are so lucky that our lives unfold without deep conflict among our projects or within our project of being moral. A life like this would certainly be one of great good fortune, but it is imaginable. In other words, the suffering that might come from the sources we have canvassed is common, but it is not necessary. A life might, in exceptional circumstances, be lived without it.

There are two sources of suffering, though, that can be avoided by no one, no matter how fortunate. They are, we might say, sources of suffering that are themselves immune to luck. This does not mean that we necessarily must suffer because of them. However, we cannot avoid being exposed to them, whether or not we do suffer in the face of them. So let us turn to a phenomenon I call "the weight of the past" and to death.

THE WEIGHT OF OUR PAST AND THE WEIGHT OF OUR FUTURE

In Eugène Ionesco's play *The New Tenant*, a man moves into a flat in London, trailed by his movers and his belongings. As the movers continue to bring in his furniture, his paintings, his lamps, and his other possessions, the flat starts to become cluttered, then crowded, then cramped. However, there is still more to be packed into the flat. Eventually objects pile upon objects, and there is hardly anywhere for the tenant to stand or sit. He asks the movers how much more there is left to bring in and is told that his belongings stretch down the stairs, the length of the street, and back to the Thames river, which is blocked with his property.

The New Tenant is a dramatic visual display of the baggage we accumulate as we move through our lives. It reminds us of the burdens, disappointments, and traumas we carry with us, but also of the hopes, accomplishments, and joys that are just as much a part of the inescapable character of who we are. It is, in short, a dramatization of the weight of our past, of the past of each of us. I would like to discuss that weight, before turning to another weight, that of our future, the ultimate future of each of us. Both the weight of our past and that of our future demise are, as the previous chapter suggests, sources of vulnerability for all of us. Unlike the sources discussed in the previous chapter, they are sources that nobody can escape. This does not mean that everyone must suffer from them. The doctrines I discuss in the following chapter seek to protect us from any suffering that might attend to the weights of the past and the future. Moreover, as we will see, we can avoid such suffering simply by ignoring these sources of vulnerability. We need not ask what might have been or what is to come. What it does mean is that, however lucky our lives may be—avoiding physical and psychological pain and limitations, conflicts of projects, and bad moral luck—we cannot avoid the weight of our past and our upcoming death as sources, if not actual producers, of suffering.

The first source, what I am calling here the weight of the past, has not often been addressed in philosophy. There are a couple of ways we might approach it. The first is through the idea of life as a narrative, or better, the goodness of life as having a narrative structure. To grasp this, consider an example of a decent life trajectory.

A woman, call her Jackie, decides to become a high school teacher. At the start of her academic career, she is uncertain of what area she would like to study. She just knows she likes kids. After a couple of false starts, she commits herself to math. Gradually, she learns math all the way through calculus, develops her teaching skills, and eventually winds up teaching in a solid high school. On another front in her life, she wonders about her sexuality. She dates men but feels drawn toward women. She would rather not admit to herself that she might be a lesbian, but eventually it becomes clear that she is sexually attracted only to other women. She meets a woman who seems at first to take care of her, but Jackie finds that this woman is increasingly possessive and eventually abusive. With difficulty she extricates herself from the relationship, which leads to a period of profound aloneness and self-doubt. However, eventually she comes to accept herself as she is, not needing someone else to affirm her. This leads her into a relationship that is more balanced and, although it too comes to an end, allows her to remain friends with the woman with whom she was involved. Although she does not have another long-term relationship with another partner, she accepts who she is and how she has come to construct her life. She would not have chosen to live otherwise.

This life displays at least two narrative characteristics that might lend it a sense of meaningfulness: it has what might be called a "rising trajectory"[1] and it displays a certain narrative coherence.[2] In her early life, Jackie has doubts about herself, both vocationally and sexually. Eventually she resolves these doubts into a worthwhile career and some intimate relationships. The fact that she resolved these doubts over the course of her life gives it a satisfying narrative structure. To put the point a bit simply, her early life presented a set of problems that her later life learned how to solve.

To see how the structure of Jackie's life lends it meaningfulness, contrast it with a life that has a descending trajectory. Imagine someone born to great good fortune whose early life seems charmed but who later, perhaps through no fault of his own, becomes destitute both financially and interpersonally. Imagine also that the sum total of goodness or happiness that this person experiences over the course of his life is the same as the sum total of happiness (or goodness, or whatever) that Jackie experiences. (You may ask here, entirely reasonably, how to measure the sum total of a life's happiness. Honestly, I have no idea. I ask you just to run with me on this one.)

Although they experience the same amount of happiness, we would probably all agree that Jackie's life is the preferable one. The reason for this lies in its narrative structure. Its rising trajectory and its coherence, where the later "chapters" build on the earlier ones, lend it a sense of significance that seems lacking in a life with a descending trajectory or no coherence. Let us now look a little more closely at Jackie's life. As it stands, while not inaccurate, the account I have given here may be overly simple in several aspects. First, let's reflect on the *content* of the narrative of this life. The woman becomes a teacher, specifically a high school math teacher. Might she ever have wondered what her life would have been like had she committed herself to being something else: an elementary school teacher, for instance, or a novelist, or an organizer on behalf of LGBT rights? And would she have gotten more satisfaction from one of these other endeavors, or perhaps met someone with whom she could have shared the entirety of her life in a deeper way? The fact is, she cannot know what any of these lives would have been like, or whether they would have been better or worse. They remain utterly foreign to her. She chose to become a high school math teacher, which is why she studies and writes and teaches what she does, and which also has a lot to do with where she lives and whom she has met. The content of her past is only one of many contents she might have chosen. While satisfied with that content, might another past have led her down other, better paths? Even the beginnings of an answer to this question remain forever barred to her. Or, to put the point another way, she may ratify her life, but, if she is self-reflective, can she do this with anything other than a certain halting recognition that she is doing so in ignorance of what the alternatives might have been like for her?[3]

The second element, what might be called the narrative

shape of a life, intersects with its content but can be considered independently of it. The shape, we might say, concerns the ups and downs of a person's life, recalling our sense of a rising and descending trajectory. Of course these ups and downs need not be so in some absolute sense; they can be the better and worse parts of one's life relative to one another. For instance, someone who is impoverished might have periods of relative material comfort that would, for a wealthy person, be experienced as destitution. Although I think that absolute levels of narrative shape are important politically, what I am more interested in here is the shape of the person's life for the one living it. This will be more a matter of relative than absolute ups and downs, although, to be sure, there are effects on the relative ups and downs of an impoverished person's life when it is lived in the midst of others' affluence.

All lives will very likely have ups and downs, but, as we have seen, in order to have more meaningfulness, there should in some sense be a rising trajectory. However, even someone whose life has a broadly rising trajectory will not be without doubts and uncertainties. To see this, we should first recognize that we never know where we are in the shape of our trajectory. This is because we cannot tell the future. One writes a book; it is a bestseller and a critical success. The present certainly looks bright, and the past commitment to writing seems vindicated. But what will the future bring? Is there another book as good as that one? Am I, the author, a one-hit wonder? Do I have any more to say? Will I look back on this moment as the writing peak of my life and, inasmuch as I identify myself as a writer, as the peak of my life as a whole? And suppose I write another one, as good as the first. How do I know there is yet another?

We can see this same dynamic in our example. The career

success of the woman is not guaranteed to continue, nor her acceptance of herself as a lesbian. Events could intervene: the closing of her high school or its consolidation with another high school that already has enough math teachers, or a wave of anti-LGBT fervor could change the shape her life radically, or the elusiveness of new ideas or loneliness could vitiate it in a more subtle way.

In a rising trajectory, the shape of the past may seem to be the right one, and rightly ordered. But nothing guarantees that what has led to the present will not be the source of longing or nostalgia later. Just as the paths not taken in the content of one's life cannot be known, neither can the future. And to the degree that the shape of a life has vindicated a particular present, from the perspective of that very present—which, as invulnerabilists are fond of pointing out, is where we always live—it can burden the future in its uncertainty. In short, the narrative shape of a life can be assessed, as many have insisted, only at the end of it. Until then, the past may be a source of disquiet in just the way that it has been a source of well-being or meaning.

There are, perhaps, lives whose trajectories are more nearly certain, but those lives are the ones that have likely peaked earlier rather than later. One thinks here, for instance, of certain National Football League players. They spend their careers gathering injuries that for many will be a source of ongoing physical suffering and limitation for the rest of their lives. While they are playing, they are often the toasts of their towns—high school, college, professional. But when their careers end and the crowds and the adoration fade, they are left with their injuries and the remainder of their days.

Turning to the third issue (after the content and shape of one's life narrative), the role of the past as at once granting or withdrawing meaning through its contribution to the shape of one's trajectory is also affected by the *current place* one occupies in that trajectory. In our example, the decision of the woman to commit herself to the study of math and pedagogy can only be justified as part of her trajectory (rather than as, say, a side road) if later events bear out that decision. Her past will be justified only on the basis of a degree of flourishing of which she cannot be certain. Alternatively, looking back on a particularly successful career and a meaningful life from near its end does not give much hope for a future that is as good. It may be that the best has happened, and what is left is no longer enjoying the continuance of an upward trajectory but rather coming to terms with its end. There is often, although perhaps not always, a sadness to the end of a good life, just as there is bitterness to the end of a regrettable one. This sadness does not withdraw the meaningfulness of a life—or at least it need not. But it is a weight associated with one's past that is inextricably bound to its positive character.

We should remind ourselves here that these various ways in which the past weighs upon a life characterize only the vulnerabilist views that are the main subject of discussion. In an invulnerabilist view, as we will see in the following chapter, only the present matters. The past can neither give nor withhold meaning or well-being. Since all that exists is the present, the past should be treated as the inexistent that it is.

So far, I have focused on the past in its place in the narrative structure of a life. I should emphasize that I don't mean to claim that all lives are narratively structured.[4] Rather, my point is that inasmuch as a narrative structure exists, it is subject to certain vulnerabilities that can disrupt the narrative. There is another angle of approach to the past, however—one that will bring into relief the themes we have discussed here in another way. This angle of approach relies on several examples. They are examples that have mostly been brought to bear in the arena of moral discussion; however, I would like to harness them to the reflect on the role of the past in a life trajectory. What brings them together is the consideration of the role of regret regarding one's past decisions.

The first example comes from the philosopher Derek Parfit.[5] Imagine a fourteen-year-old girl who is wondering whether to get pregnant. She is advised against it, being told that if she waits until she's older to get pregnant, the life of her child will be a better one. She goes against that advice, getting pregnant anyway. Her child has a difficult life but still one worth living. Since the child's life is worth living, he—the child—is glad that his mother made the decision she did. So the problem Parfit confronts is whether in fact the girl's decision to get pregnant was morally wrong and, if so, why.

The second example comes from Bernard Williams's paper "Moral Luck."[6] He imagines a Paul Gauguin, one slightly different from the historical Gauguin, who is wondering whether he should leave his family and go to Tahiti to paint. This Gaugin feels that he would be justified in going to Tahiti only if he can make a significant artistic contribution. Williams points out that the justification of his decision will depend on factors he cannot control: whether he in fact has the talent to make use of the particular sunlight in Tahiti, whether he will be disciplined enough to paint, and so on. In short, he does not know whether the contribution he makes through his painting will justify his leaving the family, and he will not be able to know until after he has left his family for Tahiti and engaged in the project itself.

In his book *The View from Here*, Wallace considers these two examples and adds a third, one that he calls the bourgeois predicament, and it settles uncomfortably upon professors like me. (We will return in depth to this example in the fourth chapter.) He points out that our ability to do what we do rests on our benefiting from various forms of exploitation that have occurred and continue to occur. Slave labor, for instance, was essential in generating some of the wealth that has been used to build universities. At many universities, lower-level jobs like those of janitors and secretaries are filled by people who have not had the educational opportunity that people like me have had access to. Moreover, they are often subject to exploitative wages, which their lack of educational opportunities bars them from rejecting and which in turn allows universities to pay higher wages to faculty. The question Wallace raises is one of whether we bourgeois professors can justify our lifestyles, given the unjust conditions on which they are built.

What I want to focus on here is not the question of whether the girl, Gauguin, or the professor are justified in the choices they have made. That is a moral question for another time. I am more concerned here with a phenomenon that Wallace calls the "affirmation dynamic," the idea that if we ratify our current situation we cannot entirely regret the conditions that gave rise to it. That is to say, if we want to endorse our lives as they are, we must also endorse the paths that led us here. We can see this in all three cases. The girl who gets pregnant, assuming she loves her child and that her child's life is worth living, cannot fully regret having gotten pregnant at an early age; she must, in the end, affirm that past. Gauguin, if he finds his work to be important or significant, cannot ultimately regret leaving his family. Finally, the bourgeois professor cannot at once affirm her life and reject the conditions on which it is based.

We should linger here a moment to see how widespread this phenomenon is. Imagine here a bourgeois professor who does not like where she lives and teaches. She is comfortable with her university life but finds the surrounding small town atmosphere politically and socially stifling. She has several children, the youngest of whom is nine years old. She has been applying for other jobs for the past twenty years but with no success. What might her attitude be toward her failure to land another job?

It would seem difficult for her, on reflection, to regret not having landed another job more than nine years ago. If she had, she would not have had this particular child. She might have had another one, but it would not have been this child, if for no other reason that it would not have been conceived under the same conditions and so would have a different genetic makeup. And, of course, her love for this child, the one she has, would identify with this child's enjoyment of his life. It is psychologically difficult, perhaps nearly impossible, for her to regret her child's existence, which entails that she must affirm her failure to find another job before nine years ago.

But there is more. Let's suppose her children are thriving. If she had been offered another job, she does not know whether they would have flourished in their changed environment. Assuming her older children are, say, under twenty or even twenty-five years old, the previous nine years include crucial periods of their development. Would they have had as good friendships or teachers or athletic companions? Would they have gotten caught up with the wrong crowd or been bullied by others for having come from somewhere else? Would one of them have suffered a debilitating injury in a car accident, which he just happened to have avoided over the past nine years where they are?

Or imagine this: during those nine years her work has received some recognition, allowing her to develop an intellectual community with others that she might or might not have developed had she found herself at another university. Would she have found anything as satisfying as that had she been chosen to work at any of the places she applied?

It is not that she cannot have any regret for not having landed a better position over past nine years but rather that that regret must be tempered by a recognition that there are uncertainties that attend to an alternative future that must diminish the intensity of the regret.

Of course, this uncertainty is a two-edged sword, as we have seen in our discussion of the narrative structure of a life. Just as it might have been worse to have moved, so might it have been better. She cannot know this. This point, however, cuts deeper than it would seem if we just look at the previous nine years. Our professor does not know whether, had she lived somewhere else, she would have had other children that she would have loved just as much. She does not know whether the trajectory of her children's lives in this small town will be more constrained and less enjoyable than those of the children she would have had in a more intellectually and culturally vibrant atmosphere. And, of course, although she does not know whether her intellectual and cultural life would have been better, she has at least some reason to think that it would.

None of this tips the scales toward some necessity to regret her failure. Particularly with regard to the period before the previous nine years, it would seem nearly impossible to do so. Rather, the issue is that regret is usually a comparative issue. One regrets one outcome rather than another. In our professor's case, and in the case of so many of us, however, that other outcome is unavailable to us. We cannot know what the alternative would be. As a result, the regret in question, as would any comparative affirmation, has a strange and perhaps unfounded structure. To regret or to affirm the one's past, in its most important aspects, is to do so in ignorance of that against which the regret or affirmation takes place.

In his novel *The Unbearable Lightness of Being*, Milan Kundera gives voice to some of the same issues but casts them differently. The narrator contrasts the philosopher Friedrich Nietzsche's thought of the eternal return—that everything that happens will happen again an infinite number of times—with the idea that everything happens just once and cannot happen another way. The former idea is, in the narrator's view, a thought of heaviness. Each event is weighted down with the task of infinite recurrence. "That is why Nietzsche called the idea of the eternal return the heaviest of burdens."[7] By contrast, events that are fleeting only happen once and are gone; they are lighter. And, he wonders, which is better? "The heaviest of burdens crushes us, we sink beneath it, it pins us to the ground. . . . Conversely, the absolute absence of a burden causes man to be lighter than air . . . and become only half real, his movements as free as they are insignificant."[8]

The imagery I'm invoking here moves in the opposite direction. It is precisely a past that is at once contingent and cannot be changed that burdens life with a certain weight: the weight of "what if?" We carry this "what if" with us, a "what if" that only gets heavier as the years pass and the forks taken imply more forks untaken and thus more paths that cannot be explored. To Kundera's thought of the lightness of insignificance I would like to pose the thought of the heaviness of singularity, its heft in knowing that things could have been otherwise but not knowing what that otherwise consists in.

What we have been considering with these examples is analogous to the question of the *content* of one's past in the above discussion of the narrative structure of a life, which was the first of the three issues we canvassed there. Since there is no analogy to our second consideration in that discussion, the *shape* of a life—these events, after all, are single events rather than life trajectories—we can turn to the third consideration we raised earlier: the *current place* one occupies in the trajectory of one's life. It is, of course, possible to regret what seemed important or worthwhile or meaningful at the time when looked back on later. An NFL football player can live off his memories for years, but as the memories fade and the effects of the injuries become more debilitating, one can begin to wonder whether the excitement and adulation was really worth it. One might think that a case like this would be irrelevant to the more usual situation, such as that of our bourgeois professor. However, I believe that doubt might creep in, particularly near the end of a life. We can imagine here that our professor, having spent her intellectual life in a place with which she has no connection, experiences a gnawing sense of emptiness as she grows old. She wonders whether a different environment with a more stimulating culture and a larger intellectual community might have offered a deeper source of satisfaction or meaning than she had previously allowed herself to think. Perhaps, she thinks, she should have made getting a better position a more important part of her life. This regret doesn't go so far as wondering whether it would have been better for her to move before her youngest child was born; but it may lead her to think that she would have been willing to risk a little more in the way of their development in order to have a more meaningful life herself.

While the past, then, might be a source of meaning, and

while it might be something difficult or even impossible to regret, nevertheless the past can weigh upon us in a manner that casts a shadow over the future in the same gesture by which it lights up a life. Moreover, that shadow and that light may well be in proportion to each other. This is not to say that they are equal. In a life one doesn't regret, they are likely *not* equal. Rather, the idea is that the more important the past is in its contribution to one's sense of her life, the larger the shadow is likely to loom. The reason for this is not difficult to see. If, for instance, one's career or one's children are central to one's life, a better career or a better environment for the children would also have been an improvement, if one could have had them.

However, there is an issue regarding the character of this shadow that must be addressed. If the past casts a shadow, how does it do so? It is surely not a psychological fact that all people have the thoughts I have ascribed to the people in my examples, any more than they might have had the positive thoughts about what they do not regret. These are thoughts that can come only upon reflection on one's life. And, in fact, they need not even arise then. It could well be that someone reflects on her past and yet is neither uplifted nor burdened by it. The past simply does not matter that much except as a springboard for the future. (We should recognize in passing that this is not an invulnerabilist view, since the unavailability or failure of future projects can still affect her life.) But if the past does not necessarily *seem* weighty to one, in what sense does it weigh?

One sense in which it might weigh, an indirect but still sometimes palpable one, is through a less reflective sense of unfulfillment. Something doesn't feel right, or doesn't feel as right as it might. The enthusiasm with which we once engaged our life is no longer there, or at least not to the same degree, and it is not being replaced with a sense of peace or tranquility. We become a member of that society, to one extent or another, characterized by what Thoreau called "lives of quiet desperation." This indirect sense, however, is still a psychological fact about some people, and again not something everyone experiences.

Another way in which the past weighs we might call broadly normative. By the term "normative" here I mean a matter not of what we *happen* to think about a situation but what we *ought* to think about it. Whether people happen to feel the weight of their past is one thing; whether they ought to is another question, a normative one. To see the normative issue, let's return for a moment to Wallace's affirmation dynamic. For him, to affirm the present requires a particular affirmation of the past that led there. His claim is not, of course, a psychological one about what people actually do. It is not that people who affirm their present always affirm their past. They often don't even make the connection between past and present. Rather, his claim is that, to the extent that people affirm their present, they are *normatively committed* to affirming their past. They cannot affirm their present without affirming the particular history that led to that present, because it is precisely that past that led them to this present. To affirm the present normatively requires affirming everything that led up to it, which in the case of the professor is the past of oppressive circumstances surrounding the building of the university (as well as the present of exploited workers sustaining it). That is where the moral difficulty he wants to address arises, the one that we will focus on in the fourth chapter.

The weight of the past is like this, with, as we will see in a moment, an important difference. To the extent to which a particular event or story line gives or adds meaning or well-being to a life, the aspects that make that event or that story line meaningful might have been realized better through a different trajectory coming from a different past. Therefore, to be committed to that past is to be committed, normatively if not in fact, to the possibility that another past might have been better. And inasmuch as we often don't know ourselves as well as we would like, and inasmuch as our past in general is important in offering our lives significance, this adds to the uncertainty about whether another life would have been better. And moreover, since none of us knows the future, we do not know whether the past that we have lived will diminish the future by contrast.

None of this requires that we actually undertake to affirm or reject our past or express regret or lack of it. Rather, it requires that a commitment to the importance of our past in giving meaning or well-being to our lives normatively requires a commitment (even if not actually undertaken) to the possibility that another past might have done so to a greater extent.

One difference between my claim of normative requirement and Wallace's is this: For Wallace, the affirmation of one's past is required because of its contribution to one's present. In other words, the situations of the young mother, Gauguin, and the bourgeois professor are caused by the decisions they made in the past and the particular circumstances in which those decisions were made and carried out (as well as the history that gave rise to those decisions and the contexts that supported them). The weight of our past operates differently. There is no causal contribution to the uncertainties I am discussing here, either because the imagined alternatives did not happen or at least have not happened yet (in the case where one's future is diminished relative to one's past). The commitment, then, is not of the form "Since A caused B to happen, by affirming B I must also affirm A." Rather, it is a recognition of the role uncertainty plays in a life. It is a commitment to the idea "Since X was an important source of meaning in my life, a different situation with more X would have been a better source" or "Since event or sets of events Y made my life much more worthwhile, the lack of events like Y might make my future less worthwhile," or "Since I am not sure of what would have made my life more meaningful than it is, I don't know whether doing X or experiencing Y was what I should have done rather than engaging in Z."

One might ask whether there is a simple escape from this normative commitment. One person I shared these thoughts with referred to it as the "What Me Worry?" option, in reference to the question posed by the *Mad* magazine character Alfred E. Neuman. I can't do anything about the past, this line of thought runs, and I can't even know what it would have been like had I chosen a different past. It's all very speculative. So why worry about it?

To see what the worry is, we need to return to the idea of normative commitment. We saw earlier that to think of certain ways of living as valuable implies that if another life contained more of what made those ways valuable, then it might have been more valuable. The response to the "What Me Worry?" option is the converse of that claim. That is to say, if I dismiss the value of other, better ways of living, this implies that I don't think of them as terribly valuable. But if they aren't valuable, then this further implies that the ways I am currently living aren't either, since they are instances of the same way of living. If, for instance, the professor doesn't care whether her children's lives might have been better under other circumstances, this normatively commits her to thinking that their well-being under the current circumstances doesn't matter either. To dismiss the value of what might have been commits one to dismissing the value of what actually is, because they are both the same value. But since the professor surely does care about her children's well-being, she is committed to caring about whether a different situation would have given her more of it. And this, of course, is the weight of the past.

None of our reflections here, I should emphasize, requires that we should either drop considering the past as a contributor to the well-being or meaning or significance of our lives, as the invulnerabilist or an entirely future-oriented person would do. Even less does it mean that we should strive to live worse lives, so that the future will not suffer by comparison. I have already pointed out that the contribution the past makes to our lives may well outstrip the sense of burden these uncertainties place on it. Rather, the point is that the past as a contributor to well-being or meaningfulness does not come without a cost, and that cost, precisely because it is uncertain, casts an indistinct shadow over our lives. This shadow, to be sure, is not one that we necessarily experience. However, to the extent to which we rely on our past to give us meaning, we are committed to the uncertainty that attends to the pasts that we did not live and the future that we have not yet lived.

I want to draw two initial conclusions from these reflections before turning to a different weight upon our lives, that of our inevitable future. The first conclusion is that narrative meaningfulness and what Wallace calls the affirmation dynamic that precludes regret have their other, darker side. That darker side often does not appear directly, and perhaps it sometimes does not appear at all. But it is there nonetheless, patiently awaiting our notice. And, having said that we often do not notice it, nor are we required to, we can recognize that it often does insinuate itself into our lives, even if briefly. Lying awake at night, wondering whether the choices we made were the right ones; sitting at our desk during dull moments at work, asking whether we could have done better; in the wake of personal failure, or sometimes even personal success, pondering whether this is all that can be expected from these particular choices of how to live: at these moments we glimpse the phenomenon I have been describing here.

The second, related, conclusion is that what I have been referring to as meaning or well-being or significance are not pure but instead tainted phenomena. The shadows cast by the pasts that never were and the future that is not yet do not destroy the significance of our lives for us, but they can make us realize that, in a world where certain choices preclude others and where much is contingent on things we cannot control, *this* life, however fulfilling, has its enjoyment supported by a necessary ignorance of its alternatives and its future. Perhaps we should not have expected better, and those of us who have been led astray by images of purity are too impressed by some sort of invulnerabilism or perhaps a religious tradition that promises escape from the finitudes of our existence. We are, however, beings not only of the more and the less rather than the yes and the no; more deeply, we are beings of maybe more and maybe less, unable to escape ourselves to know the character of that maybe.

How might we live with these uncertainties that taint us? What might we do to integrate them into our lives without their becoming a source of debilitating concern, sapping the meaningfulness that our lives do possess? Is there is a path to some sort of peace—or at least some sort of truce—between that which gives us meaning and that which bleeds bits of it away? If it is peace we are looking for, then invulnerabilist views will appear attractive to us; alternatively, there is the possibility of a truce, which we will consider in the fourth and fifth chapters. But our lives are not only attended by uncertainties about what might have been. They are also shadowed by a certainty that none of us can avoid.

*

That death can be a source of vulnerability to suffering is, at first glance, so obvious as to need hardly anything more than acknowledgment. Death is frightening. The idea of no longer being here is, for many of us, a source of terror. I once taught a course on death. It was, I believe, the best course I've taught in over two decades at my university. I won't be teaching it again, though. During the semester when the class met, I would often wake up in the middle of the night, sometimes in a cold sweat, sometimes in a warm one. The fact of my dying was right before me, and it held me in a grasp as sure as any the Queen of Darkness has ever been able to manage.

It is true that there is very little to say that is not obvious about the fact that death is a source of vulnerability. In fact, Socrates defined philosophy in terms of dealing with death, saying, "The one aim of those who practice philosophy in the proper manner is to practice for dying and death."[9] As we will see, invulnerabilist philosophies have as one of their central concerns that of dealing with death. But here is a question worth pondering: *why* is death so frightening to most of us? What is it about death that stops most of us in our tracks when we consider it?

There is, for one thing, the sheer fact of not being here. This sheer fact has at least two sides to it. First, there is the difficulty of imagining not being here. Our minds resist wrapping themselves around our own nonexistence. When we reflect on this, we want to ask ourselves, what is it like not to be here? How will it be for me to be out of existence? Even those convinced that there is life after death do not seem immune to this question. Of course, even as we ask it, we know there is something paradoxical about it. If we don't exist, there won't be anything it is like to be dead. But nevertheless, the question seems to press on us. And, as we will see, the Epicurean form of invulnerability will make much of this question, turning our nonexistence after death against our fear of it.

But there is more. Another side to our fear of death is what will end for us when we die. (As I typed this sentence, my first ending was "what we will miss when we die." This shows the persistence of the ideas in the previous paragraph.) And this brings us back to the idea of ourselves as creatures of projects. Humans are not generally creatures of the moment, creatures for whom the future does not matter. This is because many of the most significant involvements of our lives are, as we have seen, projects that orient our action toward the future. Our friendships and love relationships, our careers—and after our careers our participation in volunteer activities or writing or being with our grandchildren or cultivating our gardens—our hobbies, our athletic involvements: all of these are conceived not only as matters of what we are currently doing but also where they are leading us.

It is not that the present does not matter, nor the past. A friendship, for instance, is importantly rooted in a shared past and often enjoyed in a particular present. However, it is also considered as something that is ongoing, that will have a future beyond the present moment. We know this because of the pain of losing a friendship, not only through a friend's death but through misunderstanding or conflict or growing apart. We are cut off from a shared future that seemed woven into the friendship itself, not as a precise vision of what would happen but rather as an opening without particular shape but with the friend as company.

Death eliminates our projects. It does not bring them to completion or offer a closure to them. To be sure, if we know we are going to die soon we might ourselves seek to bring our projects to a close. But this would be our doing, not death's. Death simply ends them. When and where and how death will do so is uncertain. This is why death hangs over us throughout most of our lives. It is the source of the cliché that when one is born one is old enough to die. And whenever we die, unless we are able to bring our projects to a close—and how exactly does one bring a love relationship or friendship to a close?—then what death accomplishes is simply to cut off a project, annihilate the future anticipation woven into it.

It is this, alongside and perhaps more significant than the inability to conceive our not being here, that is the source of suffering death brings us. It is this vulnerability that is ours, not merely at the ends of our lives, but throughout them, another shadow that does not leave us. Because we are creatures of projects, the combination of death's inevitability and its uncertainty render us vulnerable in a way that does not characterize other animals who cannot think themselves forward into the future in the way we can.

However, although death is one of the deepest—perhaps *the* deepest—source of our vulnerability, it is also the source—and again perhaps the deepest source—of what makes our lives meaningful.

There have been, mostly in literature, a number of reflections on immortality. The most famous among them is probably Jonathan Swift's. In *Gulliver's Travels*, the Struldbrugs live forever but continue to age. They are a pathetic bunch, wizened and decrepit, shunned by their fellow creatures who put them out to pasture with minimal provisions and support. Their existence is something that very few of us would envy. If we want to have an appealing picture of immortality, then perhaps we should turn our imagination in a different direction.

A better comparison would perhaps be the immortals of Jorge Borges's aptly named short story, "The Immortal." In Borges's telling, the protagonist, Joseph Cartaphilus, finds himself among the immortals, whose landscape is dismal indeed. Although perfectly healthy, the immortals have stopped caring for themselves or others, since life has lost all urgency for them. Everything will happen of its own accord, sooner or later. Cartaphilus meets Homer in the City of Immortals and reflects that "Homer composed the *Odyssey*; if we postulate an infinite period of time, with infinite circumstances and changes, the impossible thing is not to compose the *Odyssey*, at least once."[10]

Many of us, when initially presented with an image of immortality, are drawn to it. After all, it is a way to avoid the terror of death. But have we really thought about what immortality might mean? Imagine that you will live forever. Imagine that your life will go on without cease. And, to give it the best gloss, imagine that you will do so as a healthy human being and that everyone you care about will join you in this immortal condition. Would this be a future worth having?

In order to see what is at stake, let us give this imagining some flesh. What are your favorite activities? Sports, music, reading, watching television, talking with friends, eating at interesting restaurants? Take any or all of these, and then consider doing them for five thousand years. Or ten thousand. That first ten thousand years, of course, would be only a flicker in the span of immortality. One image that captures immortality for me, one that I believe comes from earlier sages, is that of a desert the size of the Sahara. To this desert flies a bird every thousand years. This bird collects a grain of sand from this desert and flies off, only to return a thousand years later to collect another grain. When the bird has cleared all the sand from the Sahara, not even an instant of eternity will have passed. Immortality lasts, I think we can agree, a long time.

What happens to our projects, our relationships, the meaning and character of our lives over the course of immortality? They become shapeless. When there is time for everything, and perhaps everything will happen over the course of one's time, then the urgency of living is sapped. The threads tying us to our lives go slack. The philosopher Martha Nussbaum reminds us that "the intensity and dedication with which very many human activities are pursued cannot be explained without reference to the awareness that our opportunities are finite, that we cannot choose these activities indefinitely many times. In raising a child, in cherishing a lover, in performing a demanding task of work or thought or artistic creation, we are aware, at some level, of the thought that each of these efforts is structured and constrained by finite time."[11] It is not that this structure and constraint *alone* give our lives meaning. But without the finiteness of time, it is unclear that they could sustain us in the meaningfulness they possess for us mortals. As Homer concludes in Borges's "The Immortal," "Everything among the mortals has the values of the irretrievable and the perilous."[12]

One might argue here that there is so much to do in life, so many activities one can engage in, that it would be myopic to say immortality would leave our lives shapeless or bereft. After all, there are new people being born every day. There are different activities and pursuits being created all the time. Think of the video games and novels being written as you read this, the basketball games yet to be played, even the slow changing of the earth's surface. Novelty is always arising. There is always something different to do, some project to be pursued, someone else to meet. How could a person at all dedicated to life lose the intensity of living under these conditions?

This line of thought fails to appreciate the uniqueness of each of us. We cannot be just anybody. The individual trajectories of each of our lives offer each of us particular passions and interests and styles of relationships. There are certain people with whom we form deep relationships; others are just acquaintances. There are projects and engagements that stir us; others are just ways of passing time. There are places we want to see and immerse ourselves in because they resonate with something inside us, perhaps something inchoate even to us; other places are just amusing. The idea that novelty could continuously lend our lives shape misses this essential fact about us. For me, a life where what was left to do involved fishing, romance novels, racquetball, cocktail parties, and gardening would not be a life that compelled me. I would not really be living in such a life; I would just be soldiering on. It would not even feel like my life. It would feel like someone else's life into which I had just been dropped.

In order for our lives to have a sense of significance, we must die. We often avoid thinking about this because we often avoid thinking about death. Ignored or not, however, it remains a cornerstone for our living. This does not mean that we should embrace the fact of our dying. Matters are more complicated than that. There is a bit of a paradox here that we cannot escape. We cannot conclude from the fact that immortality would be bad for us that death is good. Death is not good for us, except perhaps for those among us in extreme pain or suffering. We might put the point this way: immortality is bad for us, and so is death. Or, to put it in the terms we have become used to: death is a profound source of our vulnerability to suffering, but so would immortality be.

This is the paradox of human mortality.[13] We need death to give us meaning, and yet the meaningfulness of our lives is precisely what makes death so frightening. Without death, our lives would be shapeless. Since we do in fact die, our lives often take on a shape; but once they have a shape, a meaning, who wants to die? As a philosopher, I am supposed to have a solution to this paradox. I am supposed to guide people on the narrow straits that lead between death and immortality, to navigate us through this Scylla and Charybdis into the tranquil waters of a consistent and nonparadoxical relationship to mortality. But I can't.

Death and its other, immortality, present us with a paradox we must grasp. We must at once recognize the evil to each of us that death inescapably is and yet not pine for a future that would bleed us of the reasons to fear death. We must embrace the fragility that lends our lives beauty and at the same time withdraws that beauty from us. There is no straight path, nor a crooked one, that will lead us beyond all this. Our home lies here, we might say.

There are those who seek a bid for immortality through the back door of this paradox. They argue that however many days I am granted, if I were asked at the end of that time whether I wanted another day would I not say yes? And if, at the end of that next day, I were asked again, would I not continue to say yes? And in the end, would this not be the embrace of immortality that I have just denied?

This is clever but ultimately misleading. It requires the mortality it seeks to overcome. If I am asked on a given day whether I would like another one, the background of that asking is the fact of my death. I live that day, in the hours before I am asked, as a mortal creature. I am not granted immortality; I am granted another day within mortality. And then another, and perhaps another. The framework of my life remains a mortal one. I remain someone who faces death, but with an indefinite reprieve. How long this can go on without my one day saying I have had enough of these extra days is a question for which I have no answer. However, the frame of the question presupposes the extension of a mortal life, not the granting of an immortal one. And so we are left with the conclusion that death is at once a source of vulnerability and a source of meaning, and that the two are intertwined.

As the weight of the past can confer both meaningfulness and suffering, so the weight of the future, of our future demise, can be at once a source of meaning and a source of suffering. For most of us, our lives seem inextricable from both the suffering they confer and the meaning they offer. There is not one without the other. If we are to feel the vibrancy of our existence, it must be trailed with a past that could have once but cannot now be otherwise. If we are to feel the urgency of our existence, it must come to an end. This, I am tempted to say, is the peculiar fate of human beings.

But is it inevitable? Is it really our inescapable destiny to be caught in this web that cannot but make us suffer? Must we, even as creatures of projects, be exposed to the pain that appears to be the inevitable correlate of those projects?

There are philosophies that deny this. These are the invulnerabilist philosophies I referred to earlier. They do not seek to deny our characteristics as human beings; what solace could they offer us if they did? Rather, they hope to offer us a path away from suffering, one that allows us to continue to exist as creatures of projects and of death without the vulnerability that seems attendant on these. I turn to them next, to see how they propose to do so, each in its own way. The question I will ultimately ask of these philosophies is not whether they can succeed. There is no reason to deny that Stoics, Buddhists, Epicureans, and Taoists are who they say they are. After canvassing what these philosophies offer, the question we will have to confront instead is whether, in the end, most of us would really want the invulnerability they promise.

INVULNERABILITY

Our bodies are fragile, as are our embodied minds. We are subject to moral conflict and to moral luck. We follow contingent life paths that leave behind others we cannot know. And in the end we die.

In the face of all this, we suffer: physically and psychologically, morally and spiritually. For many of us, the thought that we might not suffer, that we might be able to face our pain and loss with equanimity, is a tempting one. This temptation is not new. It is probably coextensive with humankind's existence. According to some, it is the reason for the emergence of theology. Gods (or God) help explain what seems mysterious and threatening. Following commandments of one sort or another helps ensure that we will avoid the worst forms of suffering. The afterlife offers us a way around death. Others, of course, dispute this. Theology, they insist, is not a human creation but instead a divine one. However, for many who suffer here and now, in the world of temporal existence, the temptation is not for ultimate salvation but for an end to anguish in this life, the one we are currently inhabiting.

For this, there are, in addition to pharmaceuticals, philosophies. Several of these offer the potential, even if remote, for an end to suffering. Buddhism, Taoism, Stoicism, and perhaps Epicureanism are among the foremost of such philosophical views. Buddhism, many will insist, is not so much a philosophy as a religion. It involves an afterlife in the form of karma and, over the course of time, has developed various gods. (In its historical development, so has Taoism.) However, for many who practice it now, particularly in the West, karma and deities are not at issue. Buddhism can be taken up as a philosophical approach to suffering without theological commitments.

Others may be surprised to see Stoicism and Epicureanism on the list. These are ancient philosophies. Do they still have adherents? In fact, Stoicism seems to be making a bit of a comeback these days. A week before I began drafting this chapter, the philosopher Massimo Pigliucci contributed a piece called "How to Be a Stoic" to the *New York Times* philosophy blog, *The Stone*.[1] It was heavily shared and received numerous positive comments. There are many points of contact between Stoicism and Buddhism that will emerge in this chapter that may make the former attractive to those who have embraced the latter. As for Epicureanism, well, I'll admit that its popularity is thin. However, rightly understood (as the opposite of what has come to be called an epicurean—that is, a lover of fine things), it is a philosophy that deserves to stand alongside the others as a candidate for invulnerability. However, I will argue that it's not clear that Epicureanism is an invulnerabilist doctrine in the same way Buddhism, Taoism, and Stoicism are. But that is for later.

There are two questions we must ask here. First, how and in what ways do these doctrines offer us invulnerability to suffering? What is the peace and equanimity they promise? Second, is that invulnerability something we would want? Of course, there will be at least *some* who would want it, so if the question is whether nobody would want it, the answer is going to be no. Rather, we must ask what an embrace of one or another of the doctrines would require as the price for not suffering, and whether most of us would be willing to pay it.

As we approach these doctrines, we of course cannot consider any of them in their full scope. Buddhism in particular has developed a number of distinct schools with a number of distinct metaphysical commitments. Within the major division of Buddhism—Theravada and Mahayana—there are the Pure Land school, the Lotus school, Vajrayana Buddhism, and of course Zen Buddhism, among many others. Moreover, aspects of Buddhism have been taken up by philosophers of mind, practitioners of health, cosmologists, and others. What we are interested in regarding these views is *solely their position in relation to the end of suffering*. In the case of Buddhism, this will bring us back to its core doctrine of the Four Noble Truths. Similarly, in Taoism we will restrict ourselves to the two classic texts, the *Tao Te Ching* and the writings of Chuang Tzu; with Stoicism, the more practice-oriented *Meditations* of Marcus Aurelius and Epictetus's *Enchiridion*; and with Epicureanism, the remains of Epicurus's own writings. This will allow us to focus on the central invulnerabilist aspects of these views. These aspects, which inform later versions of these doctrines and offer the relief from suffering that often motivates their adherents, would give a reason for those who are troubled by what we have discussed in the first two chapters to take seriously what these doctrines propose.

*

The centerpiece of Buddhism is the Four Noble Truths. In "The Legend of the Buddha Shakyamuni," an early biography of Buddha from the poet Ashvaghosha, it is rendered from the Buddha's mouth this way: "And so I came to the conviction that suffering must be comprehended, its cause given up, its stopping mastered, and this path developed."² A more contemporary summary gives us this: "(1) all life is inevitably sorrowful, (2) sorrow is due to craving, (3) sorrow can only be stopped by the stopping of craving, and (4) this can be done by a course of carefully disciplined conduct, culminating in the life of concentration and meditation led by the Buddhist monk."³ The fourth Noble Truth is also given as the Eightfold Path, a path of conduct to which we will return.

How are we to understand these truths? Why is life sorrowful in the first place, and how can this sorrow be ended? To answer these questions, we must take a quick and admittedly general glimpse at Buddhist metaphysics, at how Buddhism sees the constitution of the world.

In the Buddhist view, everything changes, dissolving and becoming something else. (We will leave aside here for a moment the issue of karma and the transmigration of souls.) There is no permanence in the universe, only the appearance of permanence. "All things in the universe may also be classified into five components or are mixtures of them: form and matter, sensations, perceptions, psychic dispositions or constructions, and consciousness or conscious thought."⁴ These things are constantly in flux. Where we see a world of more or less stable entities, what in fact exists is a process of change in which nothing remains constant.

This idea might seem foreign to us—after all, aren't there tables and chairs, and more important aren't I here? But we can begin to get a sense of it if we think in longer historical periods. The table did not always exist. Before it there was wood, and before that there were soil and nutrients. Moreover, the table will not always be here. Eventually it will break or rot and will turn into something else. What we call a table, then, is only a moment in a larger process of change. And that larger process, not the impermanent table, is the truth of things.

More disturbing to some, what goes for the table also goes for me. I have not always been here, and I will not always be. An image that is sometimes used in both Buddhism and Taoism is this: I am like a wave on the sea. While the wave rises I appear to have some independent existence. However, I am just a movement of the sea, and my death is nothing but a crashing of water into water. My truth is that I am of the sea, and as a wave I appear independent of it only for a moment. To put the point another way, for Buddhism there is ultimately only one process, which is sometimes called the One or Emptiness and sometimes Nonduality (where we think there are opposites, there is only Oneness). I am part of that One or Emptiness or Nonduality—although even the idea of a "part" can be misleading here. We might say I am of this One, so much so that there is no I there, only the One. Failing to see the One, I take myself to be an independent being, something that exists apart from the process of flux and change that is the One.

The sorrowfulness of life is grounded in the failure to recognize that the universe is a process and thus to become attached to things that are actually just passing moments of this process. One Buddhist scripture offers a pithy summary of this failure: "Ignorance is the cause of the psychic constructions, hence is caused consciousness, hence physical form, hence the six senses, hence contact, hence sensations, hence craving, hence attachment, hence becoming, hence birth, hence old age and death with all the distraction of grief and lamentation, sorrow and despair."[5] Let us unpack this passage, since it can be read in at least two ways, one of which suggests the nature of suffering and the other the path to enlightenment.

The first reading finds in ignorance the process of attachment to things and following from this, despair. There are things in the world to which I become attached, thinking that they are more permanent than they are. I am attached to material things because I fail to recognize that, like the table, they are only a part of a process of change and flux. I am attached to other people, and ultimately to myself, both of which involve the same failure of recognition. We are all part of the flux of life and death. To become invested in anything within the flux stems only from ignoring the flux itself and, more deeply, the Emptiness or the One that is the source of that flux.

The second reading points, albeit indirectly, toward enlightenment. It does so through the vexed concept of transmigration and rebirth. We are reborn precisely out of our ignorance of process, which in turn leads us to attachment. If we achieve nonattachment, then we will not be reborn. Nonattachment is what Buddhism calls nirvana. It is the culmination of the withdrawal of one's investment in the world. As one lets go of the world, one's soul, which has had its existence sustained through many lives through its attachment, is fully dissolved into the Emptiness or the One.

This understanding of nirvana requires the transmigration of souls and is also the basis for karma. Karma, of course, is the doctrine that the state of one's rebirth is determined by how close one has come to nirvana in the previous life, which in turn is determined by the extent to which one has followed the Eightfold Path. The transmigration of souls, however, might seem to violate the Buddhist idea that everything returns to the flux of the One. But it does not. Recall that we are like waves on the sea of the One, of what might also be called Being. (There are a number of terms that can be used to refer to the cosmic process.) If we believe that there are both bodies and souls, then it is possible to consider that a particular body "returns" to Being more quickly than a soul. Or, to put this elusive thought another way, the dissolution of the body occurs before the dissolution of the soul, and therefore the soul must transmigrate to a new body in a process of rebirth. The soul dissolves when it achieves nirvana.

It is possible to embrace much of Buddhism without endorsing either the doctrine of karma or the transmigration of souls. Buddhism would, on this account, still offer a vision of the cosmos in which one seeks nirvana. The only difference would be that achieving nirvana would be an individual matter and would occur only within the course of one's particular life. At the dissolution of one's body, one will have achieved nirvana or not. That is the end of the matter either way. This approach would abandon the dualism of body and soul characteristic of traditional Buddhism and, as we will see, bring it closer to Taoism.

It is not difficult to see that nirvana, as a state of nonattachment, involves chiefly the end of suffering. Recall the lesson of the Four Noble Truths: we suffer because we crave; if we end craving then we will end suffering. Nirvana is the end of suffering because it is the end of craving, of attachment to things. As one rendering of Buddhism has it, "He who maintains the doctrine of Emptiness is not allured by the things of this world, because they have no basis. He is not excited by gain or dejected by loss. Fame does not dazzle him and infamy does not shame him. Scorn does not repel him, praise does not attract him. Pleasure does not please him, pain does not trouble him."[6] Even death is not troubling, since it is only part of the process of the Being, Emptiness, the One, or again the Void. In short, reaching nirvana is the achievement of invulnerability to suffering.

How does one reach nirvana, then? What is the Eightfold Path? It can be listed as Right View, Right Intention, Right Speech, Right Action, Right Livelihood, Right Effort, Right Mindfulness, Right Concentration. However, we can condense this path into three areas: the first two concern wisdom, the next three concern ethical conduct, and the final two address concentration. One must know the Four Noble Truths, act well, and meditate. To know the Four Noble Truths is an obvious directive. If one is to cease suffering, one must know what causes it and how to go about addressing that cause. The third area, for people even only passingly familiar with Buddhism, will also strike a familiar note. Our minds are focused on the world, caught up in the appearances it presents to us. This, in turn, can lead to desire or craving. Those appearances—form and matter, sensations, perceptions, and so on—seem to us to be what there is, and we come to care one way or another about them. We forget about the One, the Void, or Being.

In order to recall oneself to Being, one must still the mind, give it an opportunity to withdraw from its attachment to the world. That is what meditation does. With practice, it stops the mind's natural inclination to attach itself to the world, which in turn diminishes and eventually ends desire. Craving, and with it oneself, are extinguished. (In fact, the word *nirvana*, literally translated, means "blown out.") Although it may seem superficially that in Buddhist meditation a person turns from the world toward herself, for instance in being told to concentrate on her breathing, that would be a misleading characterization. Meditation is not a turn from the outer to the inner but instead more simply a practice of the gradual slackening of attachment to the outer. To concentrate on breathing, for example, serves to give the mind an object of focus that will allow it to withdraw from its more natural inclination to focus on the world. (Another way to put this point, one that intersects with some of the doctrines to follow, is that by concentrating on his breath a man places himself more squarely in the present rather than dwelling on past events or his hopes and expectations for the future.) This is why, when, as often happens to beginners, attention wanders toward the world and toward desire, students of meditation are told not to worry about this and advised simply to return to focusing on breathing. Focusing on what is or is not being accomplished through meditation would be a way of returning to desire through the back door. (Some forms of Zen meditation are exceptions to this more gentle approach, since they can involve more forceful means of returning focus to one's breathing or to a koan—a phrase or saying on which one should concentrate. However, they remain committed to the central purpose of meditation.)

We might wonder, however, given the orientation of Buddhism, about the importance of the second area, ethical conduct: Right Speech, Right Action, Right Livelihood. It might seem a contradiction to be told both that attachment to the world must be overcome and that one must act properly in that world. And, as many have commented, Buddhists are particularly concerned with ethical conduct toward others. As one Buddhist poem advises, "A man's mind should be all-embracing / Friendliness for the whole world / All-embracing, he should raise in his mind / Above, below, and across / Unhindered, free from hate and ill-will."[7] How can we reconcile this with a doctrine that emphasizes detachment as the key to nirvana? There are at least two ways.

First, in engaging in ethical conduct, one is practicing to become less egoistic. If the self is an illusion, it is an illusion whose concern for itself motivates much of our behavior. The cravings we have are often caught up with self-advancement or with satisfying desires for our own well-being. Shifting attention toward the well-being of others is a way to distance ourselves from those cravings. To be sure, such focus must be done without cravings for the well-being of others—that would not rid us of such cravings, only transfer them—but ethical conduct is a good way to practice overcoming some of our strongest attachments to the world.

Second, ethical conduct is premised on the idea that we are all "part" of the same Being or One. We are not actually separate from one another; we are all aspects of the same process. Therefore, we have no reason to privilege our own well-being over that of any other creature. Ethical conduct is an expression of this recognition. This is why compassion plays such a central role in Buddhist thought. Compassion, as we will see momentarily, is not a form of desire or craving. Instead it is a way of recognizing that others are no less worthy of our attention than ourselves in a cosmos in which none of us are actually independent creatures but rather temporary manifestations of Being or the One.

In fact, it is the particular form compassion takes that is one of the key differences between the two major strains of Buddhism, Theravada and Mahayana. In Theravada Buddhism, nirvana is largely an individual goal. One seeks, perhaps over many lifetimes, to be an *Arhant*, a "worthy" or "perfect" being. An *Arhant* is not reborn because, having lost attachment to anything in the universe, she is free to exit the suffering of life. As Buddhism developed, to many the goal of individual salvation began to seem selfish. If someone was in a position to achieve nirvana, why not help others to do so? Why not extend compassion by putting off the exit from rebirth in order to help others in their struggle against craving and desire? This thought led to the emergence of Mahayana Buddhism, "Mahayana" meaning "greater vehicle." In contrast to the figure of the *Arhant*, Mahayana poses the figure of the *bodhisattva*, the one who puts off nirvana, sacrificing ultimate salvation in order to assist others until all have achieved it.

It might seem that with Mahayana Buddhism there is a step away from invulnerabilism. In contrast to the *Arhant*, the *bodhisattva* does not seek to make herself immune from the world's predations by removing herself from her own desire. Instead, she immerses herself in the world, taking on the suffering of others in order to ensure that they have an opportunity for salvation. And, indeed, there are passages in Buddhist scripture that would reinforce such a view. One passage, from the seventh century CE, testifies that "All creatures are in pain . . . all suffer from bad and hindering karma. . . . All that mass of pain and karma I take in my own body. . . . I take upon myself the burden of sorrow. . . . I must save the whole world from the forest of birth, old age, disease, and rebirth. . . . For all beings are caught in the net of craving, encompassed by ignorance, held by the desire for existence."[8] This seems to be the opposite of an invulnerabilism, one that asks of the *bodhisattva* not to rise above the predations of existence but rather to immerse herself in them for the sake of others.

However, seeing things this way would be misleading for two reasons. First, even if the *bodhisattva* took on the sufferings of others, this would not be the goal of Mahayana Buddhism. The goal does not differ from that of Theravada Buddhism: to end craving and thus achieve nirvana. Taking on the suffering of others would only be a means to ensure that all achieve a position of invulnerabilism. We might say then that for Mahayana Buddhism invulnerabilism is a collective goal rather than an individual one.

But we can go further. What is it for a *bodhisattva* to take on the sufferings of others? It may seem, at first glance, as though it would be a matter of suffering alongside others. However, this is unlikely. If the *bodhisattva* is close enough to nirvana to be able to assist others in getting there, it is because she has already developed a high degree of detachment herself. Recall that suffering comes from craving. The *bodhisattva* is near the end of her craving and therefore near the end of her suffering. Her compassion for others, then, is accompanied by an equanimity that allows her to take on the suffering of others without adding to her own suffering.

In fact, we might go further and argue that it is only because of her equanimity that she can do this. We know from experience that the deeper our own suffering, the more difficult it is to relate to that of others. A person grieving a lost loved one or the news of his own personal tragedy is not well positioned to "take upon myself the burden of sorrow" of others. Rather, it is someone who has a greater sense of balance at the moment who is more easily positioned to do so. Moreover, the idea of taking on the sorrow of the whole world cannot mean to take it on as one's own personal suffering. No one can do that. What one can do, perhaps, with enough equanimity, is not be burdened by the suffering of others so that one can assist them in theirs. The earliest biography of the Buddha, cited earlier, reports him as saying, "Having myself crossed the ocean of suffering, I must help others to cross it. Freed myself I must set others free. This is the vow which I made in the past when I saw all that lives in distress."[9]

For Mahayana Buddhism, then, as for its counterpart, Theravada, invulnerability is the goal. Detachment from desire, rising above being tossed about on the waves of the world's vicissitudes, the blowing out of one's soul: these are what Buddhism asks us to strive for. This does not mean that Buddhists do not have compassion for others; Buddhism is notable precisely for such compassion. However, this compassion stems not from a place of sympathy in which a person takes on for herself the suffering of others but instead from a place of equanimity in which she can maintain her distance from it. We must ask whether, for most of us, this goal is an attractive one. But before doing so, we need to canvass other doctrines that counsel invulnerability, in order to see their common threads.

*

When I was young, I thought of Taoism as Buddhism with a smile. It turns out that this is not really accurate, in several ways. First, Buddhists are eminently capable of smiling. Second, I've met Taoists for whom smiling seems a bridge too far. Third, as close as Buddhism and Taoism are, they remain distinct doctrines. The reason for my mistake was simple. I read Taoism mostly through the writings of Chuang Tzu rather than Lao Tzu. Chuang Tzu's writings have a lightness and humor that belie their depth of understanding.

An example is a famous story from Chuang Tzu often called "Three in the Morning." "When a monkey trainer was handing out acorns, he said, 'You get three in the morning, and four at night.' This made all the monkeys furious. 'Well, then,' he said, 'you get four in the morning and three at night.' The monkeys were all delighted. There was no change in the reality behind the words, and yet the monkeys responded with joy and anger. Let them, if they want to."[10] The story is simple, and it stays in the mind. Yet it points to the fact that many of us seek changes in our lives that do not matter: praise from the boss, a slight raise in pay, a better neighborhood restaurant, nicer clothes, friendlier salespeople at the store.

Taoism comes from Tao or Dao: the Way. At the beginning of the classic *Tao Te Ching*, Lao Tzu tells us, "The way that can be spoken of / Is not the constant way; / The name that can be named / Is not the constant name."[11] In some sense, all of Taoism boils down to this: the Way and language. Sometimes the Way is called the One, as when Lao Tzu says, "Heaven in virtue of the One is limpid; / Earth in virtue of the One is settled; / Gods in virtue of the One have their potencies. . . . It is the One that makes these things what they are."[12] What is this One, this Way that cannot be named? The question seems paradoxical at first. If the Way cannot be named, then how can we even ask what it is? It seems to be an elusive something that somehow gives rise to everything. And in a fashion, this is correct. However, we can approach the question indirectly through language.

Language predicates a particular quality of something. That is not all it does, but for our purposes it's enough. One says, "This is red" or "That is good" or "The food is tasty." But let us recall the One of Buddhism, the One of which particular things are only temporary manifestations. If we import this idea into our understanding of Taoism, we know that what is red will not always be red. (Historically, the two doctrines originated independently, but they share the view of the cosmos as a process.) Eventually the red will dissolve and become something that is not red. Likewise, what is good will pass away and what is tasty will no longer be so soon after I have tasted it. "So," as Chuang Tzu says, "all creatures come out of the mysterious workings and go back into them again."[13] To posit particular qualities of things is to miss the fact that these qualities are only temporary manifestations of the process that gives rise to them and to which they will return. We might call this process the Way or the One.

If this is right, then the Way cannot be named, since every name is a predicate and every predicate only characterizes a particular manifestation of the Way at a particular time, but not the Way itself. In fact, the Way, since it gives rise to all manifestations, might be called blue or green as well as red, bad as well as good, revolting as well as tasty. Language, in its use as predication, cannot capture the Way, which in this sense remains nameless. This does not mean that one cannot talk about the Way, only that one cannot name it. Discussion of the Way has to be indirect.

All of this might sound very mysterious, and at times the term *mystery* appears in both Lao Tzu and Chuang Tzu. However, there is a more contemporary analogy that I have often used in thinking about Taoism that makes it both more comprehensible and more plausible. We can think of the Way in terms of the environment. I am born and have my existence on this earth like a lot of other creatures. Eventually, I will die and return to the earth. Even if I am buried in a casket, sooner or later that casket will rot and my bones will be absorbed by the earth. Or perhaps a natural event like an earthquake or a flood will carry my body parts away. One way or another, I will disappear and become part of the process of the earth's changing character. Chuang Tzu captures this idea when he relates a story of Master Li's visit to Master Lai while the latter is dying. While Master Lai's family is grieving, Master Li says to them, "Shoo! Get back! Don't disturb the process of change!" Turning to Master Lai, he offers this: "How marvelous the Creator is! What is he going to make out of you next? Where is he going to send you? Will he make you into a rat's liver? Will he make you into a bug's arm?"[14]

What goes for me or for Master Lai goes for everything, from the animate to the inanimate. Mountains rise and fall; rivers change their course or dry out; the earth will eventually be absorbed by an expanding sun that will itself become a black hole. The Way is the process of the universe. It is like the One or the Void of Buddhism, however it is without karma or rebirth. And because the Way is without karma or rebirth, Taoism does not require either the ascending self-discipline over many lives of Theravada Buddhism or the *bodhisattva's* assistance to others in achieving nirvana characteristic of Mahayana Buddhism.

How, then, is a person to conform to the Way, to live within the recognition that the Way contains everything, gives rise to everything, and that everything returns to the Way? The theme that most often appears in both the *Tao Te Ching* and Chuang Tzu's writings is that of *wu-wei*, often translated as "inaction" or "nonaction." From Lao Tzu we are told that "the sage keeps to the deed that consists in taking no action and practices the teaching that uses no words."[15] Similarly, Chuang Tzu advises in his usual humorous fashion, "The one and what I said about it make two, and two and the original one make three. If we go on this way, then even the cleverest mathematician can't tell where we'll end, much less the ordinary man. If by moving from nonbeing to being to being we get three, how far will we get if we move from being to being? Better not to move, but to let things be!"[16]

But what, then, is this letting be, this inaction that is commended to us? Is it just sitting around, letting the world go on about its business and watching the passing show? For Taoism, the issue lies deeper than that. It lies closer to Buddhism's embrace of the end of craving. Rather than doing nothing, Taoism recommends accepting the universe as the process it is. It involves saying yes to everything without chasing after the illusions of permanence that the snares of language lead us to believe exist. "Therefore I say," Chuang Tzu tells us, "the Perfect Man has no self; the Holy Man has no merit; the Sage has no fame."[17] Taoism does not ask us to abandon doing things; rather, it asks us to abandon the striving, the desire, that accompanies the doing of things. It asks us to do so because once we recognize that our striving comes from the normative categories inherent in our language, and that our language leads us astray from the Way, which encompasses all the oppositions that language seeks to separate out, we are free to accept everything as it is while at the same time doing whatever it is that we do.

In this sense, Taoism is at once more serene and less morally centered than Buddhism. This is not to say that it does not have effects that we might welcome morally. When someone is less attached to herself and more relaxed in her relation to the universe, her attention can go outward, toward others. Although it denies the reality of a self just as deeply as does Buddhism, Taoism can, ironically perhaps, promote a sense of security. A person is part of a larger process, and whatever she does, she will still be part of that. There is no shame in becoming a rat's liver or a bug's arm after she dies. And so, while it lacks the precepts of ethical conduct characteristic of Buddhism, Taoism invites us to abandon self-concern in a way that allows for concern for others and for the world as a whole.

The acceptance characteristic of Taoism can be illustrated by another of the paradoxical stories that Chuang Tzu tells, this one about Carpenter Shih and a tree that he disdains because it is useless. When his apprentice asks him about the tree, Shih scoffs. "It's a worthless tree! Make boats out of it and they'd sink; make coffins and they'd rot in no time. Use it for doors and they would sweat sap like pine; use it for posts and the worms would eat them up." Later, the tree comes to Shih in a dream and tells him, "I've been trying for a long time to be of no use, and now that I'm about to die, I think I've got it. This is of great use to me. If I had been of some use, would I ever have grown this large?"[18] A few pages later, Chuang Tzu has one of his characters say, "All men know the use of the use of the useful, but nobody knows the use of the useless!"[19]

What is the use of the useless? In one sense, the question seems an odd one, and Chuang Tzu is pointing us toward that. It recalls us to the snares of language. The Tao generates both the useful and the useless, and to value the useful over the useless is to fail to grasp this truth. If we allow ourselves a little imprecision with language, however, we can see that there is another point Chuang Tzu is driving at. The old tree does not strive to become useful; it does not seek to be anything in particular that might be helpful to Carpenter Shih. It just *is*. It has achieved the status of letting things be, including itself. And in this way, it stands as a lesson to others, including Carpenter Shih in his dream, just to let things be, not to seek to be this or that or, as Taoism sometimes says, any one of the ten thousand things. This, it might be said, is the use of the useless.

With this we can see the particular invulnerabilist character of Taoism. Chuang Tzu remarks, "Joy, anger, grief, delight, worry, fickleness, inflexibility, modesty, willfulness, candor, insolence—music from empty holes, mushrooms springing up in dampness, day and night replacing each other before us, and no one knows where they sprout from. Let it be! Let it be! [It is enough that] morning and evening we have them, and they are the means by which we live."[20] Taoism calls us to be at peace with everything that happens, to keep a distance from ourselves and our emotions, not to be gripped by the false dualities that language places before us. Everything and its opposite emerge and then disappear. What is important is to recognize this process and then to let that recognition loosen our grip on the world and its grip on us. This is not exactly, as in Buddhism, to achieve a state of nirvana that will allow us to end the cycle of birth and death. Since Taoism (at least in its traditional philosophical form) has no notion of an immaterial soul—and in this way it also accords with a more contemporary environmentalism—it has no notion of rebirth. One is born, one dies, one merges with the earth, nourishing and thus becoming part of something else.

However, the serenity offered by Taoism is not entirely foreign to nirvana. In removing oneself from the snares of language, one also abandons desire and craving, and through this one comes to the kind of peace that such detachment brings. "If you are content with the time and willing to follow along," Chuang Tzu advises, "then grief and joy have no way to enter in."[21] While the metaphysics of Taoism—its rejection of rebirth and thus its view of our place in the universe—may be distinct from that of Buddhism, the goal of equanimity in the face of all things is close kin. Remove the Buddhist idea of karma and rebirth, which we suggested above is the way many

Westerners take up Buddhism in any event, and the two draw even closer. When someone disengages his emotional gears from the gears of the world, he passes beyond suffering to a place of imperturbability. Physical pain and the losses it entails are simply that and no more. Psychological pain diminishes. Moral quandaries and conflict are nothing more than moments in a larger process. The weight of the past drops away, since he need not wonder what else might have been. What happens is what there is, and there is nothing else besides. Even death loses its fearful character, since a life is just an instant of a process from which he has come and to which he will return.

We in the West have often associated Eastern thought with such ideas, if not with the idea of invulnerability generally. It often seems to us that the contrast between Eastern and Western philosophy is that the former is about peace and serenity while the latter struggles with concepts and precision. However, if we turn to a couple of ancient Western philosophies, we will see that, although their paths are very different from those of Buddhism and Taoism, they lead us to an invulnerabilism that would not be foreign to their Eastern counterparts. This is especially true of a philosophy that, at first glance, might seem to be utterly alien to the compassion of Buddhism or the humor of Chuang Tzu's Taoism.

*

The Stoics often repeated, with approval, the response that the ancient Greek philosopher Anaxagoras gave when he learned of his son's death: "I always knew that my child was a mortal." That image, perhaps, sums up what many of us think of when we hear the name of Stoicism. It is a resigned, dour philosophy that teaches us to bear up—to man up, in current gendered parlance—in the face of a miserable world. Life is suffering, the Stoics tell us, and we had best get used to it. Face it with dignity but without humor; don't be ground down, but don't get your hopes up very high either. The victory lies in getting over life rather than in living it.

Although it is entirely in keeping with Stoicism to endorse Anaxagoras's reaction to his son's death, the idea of Stoicism as a resignation or a bearing up in the face of an indifferent or even cruel cosmos is mistaken. In some ways, that idea is the opposite of the Stoic belief. In order to understand Stoic invulnerability, we must first grasp that, for the Stoics, the universe is entirely rational. Nothing happens that should not happen. As the great Stoic philosopher Marcus Aurelius wrote to himself in his *Meditations*, "Providence is the source from which all things flow; and allied with it is Necessity, and the welfare of the universe. You yourself are a part of that universe; and for any one of Nature's parts, that which is assigned to it by the World-Nature or helps to keep it in being is good."[22] Far from being barbarous or even pointless, the universe is as it should be. Anaxagoras's reaction to his son's death was, for the Stoics, far from an example of proper resignation. It was instead a model of acceptance and even affirmation of an ultimately rational universe.

The idea of a rational universe is foreign to many of us. Rather than rational, it seems at best indifferent or arbitrary. There is evil, both natural and human. There are tragedy, accident, unfairness, and pointless cruelty. Nature itself seems a dominion of insensitivity, where creatures survive by preying upon those that cannot resist them. To embrace the idea of a rational universe seems an act of willful ignorance rather than an exercise in philosophical wisdom.

The Stoics, of course, were not the only philosophers to face this problem. Later, in Christianity, it became known as the problem of evil. How is it, Christians have asked, that a benign and loving God could allow for the existence of evil? Many of the answers given to this problem have seemed inadequate. For instance, the common idea that evil flows from human free will, and that it is better that humans have free will than not, fails to account for natural evils like earthquakes or hurricanes as well as for the death of infants and small children. At times, the response to this is that God works in mysterious ways. However, that response is not available to Stoicism, since rationality cannot be a mystery. It must be, well, rational.

Stoicism approaches this problem from another angle. Rather than taking up the problem of evil, it instead takes up the problem of living. How is one to live in a world in which there is pain and suffering, in which things often don't seem to work out, and in which even the best lives encounter insuperable obstacles? If the universe or the cosmos is rational, at least it will not set before us tasks we cannot master in our living, hurdles we cannot clear in order to live a good life.

And this is precisely what the Stoics believe. The universe will not place before us tasks we cannot accomplish. It will not, or at least need not, push us beyond our limits. A good life is available to all of us. The question, then, is one of how to live it.

This question is inseparable from another one: what can I control? If the good life is available to all of us, then whatever it is that constitutes a good life must be under our control. For the Stoics, it is. There is much that we cannot control in the world. We cannot dictate what others do. We cannot control the workings of the natural environment. We cannot even determine the health of our bodies. We might contribute to our bodies' greater health by exercising and eating well, but nevertheless our bodies are subject to disease and injury about which we often can do very little. We might summarize all this by saying that we cannot control how the world unfolds. What we can control, however, is our *relation* to the world—that is, how we take up the world in our own existence. This is where the Stoics place their philosophical stake.

The Stoic philosopher Epictetus sums up the core idea: "Straightaway then practice saying to every harsh appearance, You are an appearance, and in no manner what you appear to be. Then examine it by the rule which you possess, and by this first and chiefly, whether it relates to the things which are in our power or to the things which are not in our power: and if it relates to anything which is not in our power, be ready to say, that it does not concern you."[23] The foundational goal of Stoicism, then, is to control one's reactions to the world, recognizing that they are the only things one can control. If this seems a pessimistic view, it shouldn't. Recall that for the Stoics, the universe is a rational one, and that part of its rationality is that it is not constructed in such a way as to bar us from living a good life.[24] If this is so, then a good life must consist only in things we can fully control. Finally, if all that we can fully control is our relation to the world, then that must be what a good life consists in.

The question then becomes one of what relation we are to take to the world in order to remain in control of what we can control. Here again the Stoic answer is straightforward: we should accept what happens. We should not be disturbed by the things that occur around or to us. This does not mean that we should not try to act well (we will return to that idea shortly). Rather, it means that, regardless of what we seek to do, we should accept with equanimity everything that actually does happen. As Epictetus tells us, "Seek not that the things which happen should happen as you wish; but wish the things which happen to be as they are, and you will have a tranquil flow of life."[25]

Stoic tranquility, then, is an achievement that consists in abandoning the desire for things to be a certain way in the name of an acceptance of the way things are. Already we can see affinities with both Buddhism and Taoism. With Buddhism there is the commendation to end craving, since craving seeks "that the things should happen as you wish." And with Taoism (and Buddhism as well) there is a serenity that emerges when one stops insisting on "three in the afternoon" rather than "three in the morning." And there is more. For Stoicism, as Marcus notes, the rationality of the universe does not imply stability or stasis. After he remarks on one's helping to keep World-Nature good, he immediately goes on to say, "Moreover, what keeps the whole world in being is Change: not merely change of the basic elements, but also change of the larger formations they compose."[26] The universe, while rational, is not a monolith. It is for Stoicism, as for Buddhism and Taoism, a process, one that maintains itself through change rather than stagnation.

Much of Stoicism as it appears in Epictetus and Marcus consists in exercises whose goal is to allow its adherents to inculcate the lessons of Stoicism. In Marcus's case in particular, this is not surprising. After all, the *Meditations* is not a set of lessons written for the sake of others but instead a record—and a poignant one at that—of his own struggle to become a true Stoic. In fact, the meditations themselves were exercises, daily reminders of what he needed to do, of where he had succeeded and, more often, where he had failed, of what is important and what is not important. While the exercises are various, they can all be categorized under the label of practices whose goal is to eliminate our passions in favor of our reason. From the beginning of the *Meditations*, Marcus sets for himself exercises to make himself a better Stoic. The opening lines of the second book (the first book—of twelve, totaling a little over one hundred pages—is an expression of gratitude to all those who have helped him over the course of his life) are "Begin each day by telling yourself: Today I shall be meeting with interference, ingratitude, insolence, disloyalty, ill-will, and selfishness—all of them due to the offender's ignorance of what is good or evil."[27] This is Marcus's attempt to gird his loins against his own temptation to become angry—that is, passionate—in the face of those who are what they are because they are not Stoics. To be a Stoic is to recognize this, and not to rise to the bait of one's own emotional temptation. The famous Stoic Seneca advised others to begin each day (as he did) by reminding themselves of what they need to do and how they need to be, and then to end each day by taking stock of how well they have done this. The purpose of the latter exercise is not to berate oneself for one's failures but instead to prepare oneself better for the next day.

One of Marcus's exercises concerns death, an often repeated theme in the *Meditations*. Marcus reminds himself that he will die and that his death doesn't matter. Few will remember him, and soon those few will be dead. (This, of course, turned out to be ironic, given the now classic status of the *Meditations*.) "The man whose heart is palpitating for fame after death does not reflect that out of all those who remember him every one will himself soon be dead also, and in the course of time the next generation after that, until in the end, after flaring and sinking by turns, the final spark of memory is quenched."[28]

Moreover, "living and dying, honour and dishonour, pain and pleasure, riches and poverty, and so forth are equally the lot of good men and bad. Things like these neither elevate nor degrade; and therefore they are no more good than they are evil."[29] There is no reason to fear death, since it is not a mark of failure or disgrace. It is our relationship to death, our ability to face it without losing equanimity, that matters.

In facing death, Marcus raises a consideration that bears close resemblance to Taoism. "We should apprehend, too, the nature of death;" he tells himself, "and that if only it be steadily contemplated, and the fancies we associate with it be mentally dissected, it will soon come to be thought of as no more than a process of nature."[30] In this process of nature, "every part of me will one day be re-fashioned, by a process of transition, into some other portion of the universe."[31] Whether this transition will lead him to become a rat's liver or a bug's arm, he does not say. However, the recognition of his life as a part of a larger process, for the Stoics a rational process, is designed to sap our fear of the inevitability of death. This can also be said of the above passages about being forgotten. Recall, Marcus tells himself, that everyone dies and is forgotten. That is how the universe works. Its rationality should lead us away from resistance to death.

This approach to death is also close to Buddhism, however its fit is not as tight. For Buddhists who believe in karma and reincarnation, there will be a resistance to this idea. Since most of us need many lifetimes to achieve nirvana, we cannot rest content with the idea that we will become part of the process of the universe when we die. Instead, an aspect of us will remain until we have achieved nirvana and left the cycle of death and rebirth. Alternatively, for those who embrace Buddhism without the metaphysics of reincarnation, while death should still be faced with equanimity, that facing is approached indirectly rather that straight on. For Marcus we lose the fear of death by analyzing it, having it "mentally dissected" (dissecting experiences in order that they will lose their grip is a common Stoic exercise); for Buddhists it is the stilling of the mind generally, along with ethical action and keeping the Four Noble Truths close by, that will have the effect of distancing us from the fear of death.

For Buddhism, as we have seen, fully inhabiting the present is one goal of meditation. This is what will distance us from the fear of death, which is in the future. I should note that, while Stoicism approaches death differently, the idea of inhabiting of the present is not foreign to its view. Epictetus counsels, "destroy desire completely for the present,"[32] and Marcus periodically reminds himself that "the passing moment is all that a man can ever live or lose."[33] However, while both philosophies recognize that the present is all there is, the place of the exercise of inhabiting the present is different for Stoics than it is for Buddhists. The latter have this exercise as a central element of their approach to life through meditation, while for the Stoics it is one exercise among others in learning to eliminate the passions in favor of reason.

An exercise in addition to that of coming to terms with one's own death, and perhaps a more difficult one, is that of coming to terms with the deaths of those we love. Recall the Stoic endorsement of Anaxagoras's reaction to his son's death. Epictetus offers the following advice: "If you are kissing your child or wife, say that it is a human being that you are kissing, for when the wife or child dies, you will not be disturbed."[34] Marcus echoes this sentiment. "Where he begs, 'Spare me the loss of my precious child,' beg rather to be delivered from the terror of losing him."[35] Perhaps the perceived coldness of Stoicism lies here as much as anywhere in their view. However, although Stoics are clear-eyed in their view that one ought not to grieve the loss of a loved one, this view could equally characterize both Taoism and Buddhism. In discussing Taoism, we have seen that Master Li dismissed the grieving of Master Lai's family, telling them not to disturb the process of change. And equally with Buddhism, its compassion for others need not extend to grieving. For those who believe in karma and reincarnation, there will be no loss of life but instead the granting of another one until nirvana is achieved. Moreover, the recognition that we are only waves upon the sea of Being should blunt grieving for the sake of the other while the project of ending craving should block a sense of our own loss.

In the end, then, for the Stoics, as for Buddhists and Taoists, the ultimate goal of living is invulnerability, to live a life where suffering cannot enter in. "To be a philosopher," Marcus tells himself, "is to keep unsullied, and unscathed the divine spirit within him, so that it may transcend all pleasure and all pain . . . accept each and every dispensation as coming from the same Source as itself . . . and last and chief, wait with a good grace for death, as no more than a simple dissolving of the elements whereof each living thing is composed."[36] For Stoicism, the elimination of the passions, the acceptance of everything that is, leads to a tranquility that cannot be shaken by worldly events, even the deaths of one's closest friends or relatives.

This might lead one to believe that Stoicism recommends our taking care of ourselves while lacking the compassion that Buddhism, especially in its Mahayana version, displays. This, however, would be a mistake. Like Buddhism, Stoicism recommends virtuous action toward others. Marcus counsels himself that, although a person should not be disturbed by the actions of others, "In one way humanity touches me very nearly, inasmuch as I am bound to do good to my fellow-creatures and bear with them."[37] This exhortation, which Marcus periodically repeats throughout his *Meditations*, might seem to be in tension with the rest of his Stoic view. After all, if the project of Stoicism is to accept what is, to "wish the things that happen to be as they are," what would be the point of involvement with others, or for that matter of seeking to change anything from what it already is?

Stoicism does, however, leave room for virtuous action and can indeed see it as worth doing, perhaps even a duty. Its approach would be along the line of the bodhisattva, who recognizes what a good life is and feels bound to help others achieve it. Recall Marcus's advice to himself, that he should recognize that he will meet people who will be offensive in various ways, but only because they themselves do not recognize the nature of the good. Once he has recognized that nature, why would he not share it with others? Why not help them come to peace with themselves as he is seeking to? The only difference between him and others is that he, while still struggling with himself, knows the proper goal.

This sharing, however, should be done in a proper Stoic manner. A man ought not to foist himself on others, because this would indicate that he has a need that others be a certain way, that he feels they must take heed to what he is offering. But to need others to listen to him is to fail to have properly eliminated his own passions. Instead, a man should make himself available to others, offering to them without concerning himself with whether they accept or reject his offerings. In fact, Stoics argue, it is more likely that others will be able to hear someone if he is not invested in the effects of his own actions. In his work *On Wrath*, Seneca counsels against allowing anger any place in one's deliberations, explaining that a reasoned path is always the right one. "Reason herself," he explains, "to whom the reins of power have been entrusted, remains mistress only so long as she is kept apart from the passions: if once she mingles with them and is contaminated, she becomes unable to hold back those whom she might have cleared from her path. For when once the mind has been aroused and shaken, it becomes the slave of the disturbing agent."[38]

The Stoics, then, like the Buddhists, reject disengagement from others in favor of compassion for them. However, their compassion, also like that of the Buddhists, comes from a solidarity that does not involve desire. If for the Buddhists it is the duty of a bodhisattva to help others attain nirvana, for the Stoics it is the duty of a being of reason to act in accordance with reason. Neither the Stoic nor the Buddhist (nor, for that matter, the Taoist) can be hurt by the actions of others, since it is only how one conducts oneself that matters. To rid oneself of desire, to live in the present, to focus on one's own actions and reactions, to do "what you must do that your will shall be comfortable to nature,"[39] is to be engaged with the world without being vulnerable to it. It is the common task, although differently conceived, of the three philosophies we have seen here.

*

There is, perhaps, no philosophical view so roundly misunderstood as Epicureanism. This is because the term *epicurean*, as it has come down to us, means the opposite of what it meant to Epicurus. Not that the two—the philosophy and the term—are entirely foreign to each other. They have a common root. But that root has grown into two entirely different plants.

The common root is this: the goal of life is pleasure. For both Epicurus and for what we now call epicureans, pleasure is indeed the point of living. However, all similarity between the two ends there. For epicureans, pleasure requires a refined sensibility, an ability to distinguish subtle differences, for example, in the various tastes of food so that one can enjoy each particular flavor. An epicurean pursues pleasure, seeking it out in its many guises among the manifold sensualities the world offers. I picture an epicurean, perhaps a bit unfairly, as someone who disdains common joys in favor of those inaccessible to most of us, who thinks of gourmet food and fine wine and sex as the highest goods, and who asks what life can offer him in the way of the next pleasure rather than ever stopping to ask what he might contribute. All of this would make an epicurean life the opposite of what Epicurus would recommend. "Nothing is enough," he tells us, "for whom enough is little."[40]

But if, for Epicurus, life is a matter of pleasure, then what kind of pleasure is it a matter of? What, in fact, does he mean by pleasure? Pleasure, for Epicurus, is serenity, a life that is undisturbed by needless worries and concerns. It is, we might say, a joy in living at that particular moment, one that requires very little in order to be experienced. If the epicurean seeks to amplify and complexify pleasure, Epicurus seeks to simplify it, for that is all life requires. To understand Epicurus, then, we must understand the components of a simple life, one that, while allowing for enjoyment in many forms, takes joy in the very act of living and in that way joins the philosophies we have already seen in commending tranquility in the face of the suffering life offers. (However, as we will see, with Epicurus the situation is a bit more complicated than the label of invulnerabilism would lead one to believe.)

For Epicurus, all pleasure is good, and to that extent is to be enjoyed. However, this does not mean—and here is where he departs from the epicurean—that all pleasures are to be pursued. Many of the pleasures we could pursue are bound to end in frustration, either because we don't actually get them or because they aren't all they're cracked up to be or because they satisfy only temporarily and then we must pursue them again. (Of these last, one might think of addictive drugs as an example. However, shopping for clothes also seems to have this quality.) So in thinking about pleasures, we must consider which ones are worth pursuing and which we should avoid. This leads us back to the question of desire, which, as we have seen, is central to the philosophies we have already discussed.

"One must reckon," Epicurus writes in his "Letter to Menoeceus," "that of desires some are natural, some groundless; and of the natural desires some are necessary and some merely natural; and of the necessary some are necessary for happiness and some for freeing the body from troubles and some for life itself."[41] The goal, then, is to distinguish the necessary desires from those that are either groundless or natural but unnecessary. The groundless desires will encompass many of the desires of the epicurean. They are also the desires that most advertisements seek to elicit. After all, if the desires they seek to elicit were natural, then they would not have to be elicited in the first place. I don't know of anyone, for instance, who needs—really *needs*—a Rolex or a Lexus. (For that matter, it's not at all clear to this owner of a primitive cell phone that very many people really need an iPhone. And I know some people who own them who really need *not* to own them.)

By contrast with groundless desires, natural desires are bound to arise whether or not we want them to. However, not all of them are necessary for our existence. This does not mean we cannot fulfill them if an opportunity to do so happens to come along. What this means is we should not hanker after them. "One must not force nature but persuade her. And we will persuade her by fulfilling the necessary desires, and the natural ones too if they do not harm [us], but sharply rejecting the harmful ones."[42] We might consider, among the natural but not necessary desires, the desire for sex. If an opportunity for sexual activity presents itself, and there is no harm in pursuing it, then the pleasure it offers would be worth having. However, because the desire for sex can be a strong urge, it is better in Epicurus's view to tame it than to spend time seeking its fulfillment. The latter can only end up destroying the tranquility of a life.

What, then, are the necessary desires? "The cry of the flesh: not to be hungry, not to be thirsty, not to be cold. For if someone has these things and is confident of having them in the future, he might contend even with Zeus for happiness."[43] These are the simple pleasures, or at least most of them, and, as Epicurus insists, they are easily satisfied. Hunger, thirst, and the desire for warmth are the necessary desires. To have them fulfilled—and to understand that they are all that is necessary—is to come close to having a life of tranquility. Close, but not entirely there. At least one other pleasure is necessary according to Epicurus. "Of the things which wisdom provides for the blessedness of one's whole life, by far the greatest is the possession of friendship."[44]

In addition to simple nourishment and warmth, Epicurus counts friendship as a necessary desire. It is one that brings pleasures that cannot be substituted for by anything one does alone. Sociality, then, must be counted among the necessary desires, the desires that must be fulfilled in order to have a good life. Epicurus's follower Lucretius, in his poem *On the*

Nature of Things, offers us an image of such a life when he writes, "And if the house doth glitter not with gold / Nor gleam with silver, and the lyre resound / No fretted and gilded ceilings overhead, / Yet still to lounge with friends in the soft grass / Beside a river of water, underneath / A big tree's boughs, and merrily to refresh / Our frames, with no vast outlay—most of all / If the weather is laughing and the times of the year / Besprinkle the green of the grass around with flowers."[45] This image of simple pleasures shared with others captures the good life, the one that, if we train ourselves in our desires, will allow us to live with equanimity and without suffering.

But what about death? Doesn't death hang over us as the inevitable end of all of our living? The simple pleasures themselves will come to an end, and, if those pleasures are worth having, then doesn't death, which destroys our ability to have them, remain an evil that we cannot overcome? Here is where Epicurus—as well as his student Lucretius—are at their most powerful. Epicurus admits that "one can attain security against other things, but when it comes to death all men live in a city without walls."[46] However, as he argues, this is not a problem. Death should not be a worry to us, for the same reason that a good life consists in pleasure.

"Get used to believing that death is nothing to us," Epicurus advises Menoeceus, "for all good and bad consists in sense-experience, and death is the privation of sense-experience."[47] In a stance that might be taken as the opposite of Christianity's, Epicureanism's reason that we should not fear death has nothing to do with the immortality of the soul. Because we are creatures of sensation—which is why pleasure and pain are so important—and because when we die we lose all sensation, we have nothing to fear in death. There will be nobody there to suffer pain just as surely as there will be nobody there to feel pleasure.

This is an idea that, while easy to think about in the abstract, is hard to really wrap ourselves around. When we think of our death, we often think of our "being dead." We consider ourselves as somehow still there, but dead. And we fear that state of being there but being dead. This, Epicurus tells us, is an error. When we are dead, there is nobody there to be dead. We are gone. "When we exist, death is not yet present, and when death is present, we do not exist."[48] So there is nothing to fear in death. It cannot be a bad way to be, since it is not a way of being at all.

Some might argue that death remains bad because it is a loss of life for someone who could have had more life, even more pleasure. Epicurus would claim that this is to misconceive things. Death cannot be a loss for the person who dies, since that person is no longer there. And, as Epicurus points out, it cannot be a loss for individuals while they are living, because while they are living they are not dead.

Epicurus's follower Lucretius adds two other arguments. The first has come to be called the symmetry argument, and the second we might call the "graceful exit" argument. "Nothing for us there is to dread in death, / No wretchedness for him who is no more, / The same estate as if ne'er born before, / When death immortal hath ta'en the mortal life."[49] If we don't fear or dread the time before we were born, why should the time after we die be of concern to us? Since they are both the same state, or lack of state, our attitude toward each should be the same. And since it is irrational to fear the time before we were born, it is just as irrational to fear the time after we die. Regarding a graceful exit, Lucretius reminds us that the earth can only sustain so many people, and that we need to give way to those of the next generation so that they might live as fully as we have. "Up, with good grace! make room for sons . . . For stuff must be / That thus the after-generations grow."[50] We have had our time here and enjoyed our pleasures, and if we have done so in a way that Epicurus would recommend, we should gracefully yield our place so others may enjoy the simplicity of pleasures as we have.

The arguments Epicurus and Lucretius present against fearing death have been the object of much discussion in philosophy.[51] However, our purpose here is not to assess their worth but to understand the ways in which the philosophical perspective of Epicurus seeks to inure us against suffering. If death is one of the most fearsome experiences for humans, it threatens to undo the pursuit of simple pleasures that Epicurus recommends as the good life. His (and Lucretius's) arguments against fearing death are dedicated to neutralizing that threat.

Nevertheless, someone might argue, Epicurus's view does not seem to be an invulnerabilist one. After all, there are necessary desires, and if those desires are not met, won't one suffer? Isn't one vulnerable to the world at least as far as food, sleep, warmth, and friendship are concerned? Is it not the case that a lack of these will cause us suffering since they bar us from the tranquility Epicurus recommends? And even if food, sleep, and warmth were easily obtained (and they aren't, for much of the world), doesn't friendship require the nearby existence of others who are compatible with us?

Epicurus's view here is complicated. On the one hand, it would seem that the world must cooperate, even if minimally, in order for us to avoid suffering. On the other hand, he does provide an argument whose effects would blunt the need for that cooperation. The problem with the argument is that it is not a very good one. "He who has learned the limits of life knows that it is easy to provide that which removes the feeling of pain owing to want and make one's whole life perfect."[52] But is this true? Can hunger that cannot be sated be so easily dismissed? Or sleeplessness? As I write, the United States continues to deal—or perhaps more accurately, not to deal— with its recent history of torturing prisoners. Among the most effective methods of torture, alongside such cruelties as waterboarding, is enforced sleeplessness, which can lead to temporary psychosis. And what about friendship? There are those who can live like hermits, but for most of us it is central to our flourishing to have others whom we care about and who care about us. And, as we have seen, Epicurus would agree.

It is worth noting that the Stoics have a similar view about pain, especially physical pain. However, in their case the view is more consistent with their core perspective. Marcus tells himself, "If [pain] is past bearing, it makes an end of us; if it lasts, it can be borne. The mind, holding itself aloof from the body, retains its calm, and the master-reason remains unaffected."[53] For my own part, I find this implausible. When I had my kidney stone I was in so much pain that I felt the layers of myself peeling away until all that was left was the pain itself. I suspect childbirth is not unlike this when the waves of pain roll through a woman's body. However, I am not a Stoic and therefore would not want to declare that distancing oneself from physical pain is impossible. I have heard of Buddhists who can withstand what would cause profound physical distress in others, and we have probably all learned of firewalkers from various cultures—people who walk across hot coals for religious or other cultural reasons but do not feel pain. And in the case of the Stoics, if someone can train herself not to grieve the loss of her child, then perhaps she has at least a start on coping with physical pain.

However, what matters here is that, for the Stoics, since the goal is the removal of desire, then it is at least consonant with their view that one can withstand physical pain through the elimination of the desire for its ending. This is not so for Epicurus, for whom there are, as we have seen, necessary desires. These necessary desires, if frustrated, must lead to some sort of suffering. To be sure, Epicurus has simplified the desires that must be met and so reduced the possibility for suffering. But, in contrast to the Buddhists, Taoists, and Stoics, it is not clear that his view allows for a complete invulnerabilism, although he seems to seek it. There remains a tension in his view between an embrace of invulnerability as exemplified in the passage on removing pain and the endorsement of certain desires as necessary.

Epicurus sums up his doctrine with the fourfold view that we need fear neither the gods nor death and that good is easily obtained and bad, easily endured: "Who do you believe is better than a man who has pious opinions about the gods, is always fearless about death, has reasoned out the natural goal of life and understands that the limit of good things is easy to achieve completely and easy to provide, and that the limit of bad things either has a short duration or causes little trouble?"[54] We should take this summary to reflect, contrary to what Epicurus seems to imply here and elsewhere, a vulnerabilist rather than invulnerabilist vein. Good things, as he has defined them, may be easy to achieve *most of the time*, and bad things borne with equanimity *most of the time*. But, given the requirements of his view and perhaps the character of most of our lives, not always.

*

Before asking the vital question of whether any of these doctrines offer most of us a model for living that we would want
to embrace, we should consider a contemporary version of
them. Eckhart Tolle is one of the most widely read spiritual
figures of our time. His influential book *The Power of Now* is
worth pausing over for several reasons. First, because it is so
popular. Popularity itself is no mark of merit, however, and so
the second, perhaps more valid, reason is that it offers what
seems to me a powerful doctrine of invulnerabilism. And part
of its power lies in the fact that—and this is the third reason—
it relies on many elements of the views we have canvassed in
this chapter. This reliance is, on Tolle's part, by design. He
sees his view as simply an unfolding of the wisdom that has
preceded him in various doctrines, from Buddhism to Christianity—although the connection to the latter seems to me to
be a stretch. In any event, Tolle offers a contemporary version
of invulnerabilism that has had broad appeal.

Before we begin, however, we should quickly note one essential difference between Tolle's thought and that of the earlier doctrines. Earlier forms of invulnerabilism are grounded
in different cosmological views. Buddhism grounds its view
in the One or the Void, as does Taoism in its way. The Stoics
are committed to the rational unfolding of the universe. The
Epicureans have a view of the universe that we have not discussed, but it involves a surprisingly prescient conception of
atoms. Tolle, for his part, seeks the wisdom of various doctrines but without their cosmological groundings. (He does
occasionally refer to Being, but not by way of offering a cosmological foundation for his thought.) On the one hand, this

frees him to take what he finds useful from those doctrines. On the other, he can present a sympathetic case for invulnerabilism to many who are not compelled by the cosmologies of these earlier views, such as the many practitioners of contemporary Buddhism who do not believe in reincarnation. For such practitioners, Tolle offers a way of thinking about invulnerabilism that should have resonance.

For Tolle, who went through his own spiritual crisis before coming to the view he now holds, we humans usually live with a particular problem. The way he puts it is that we live unconsciously. He sums up unconsciousness this way: "the basic mechanics of the unconscious state: identification with the mind, which creates a false sense of self, the ego, as a substitute for your true self rooted in Being."[55] Because Tolle uses language in often unfamiliar ways, it is easy to misunderstand what he is saying here. In particular, one might wonder how it is possible to live unconsciously while identifying with one's mind. The key to understanding what he is on about lies in the title of the book: the power of now. Living unconsciously, that is, through our mind, is how we fail to recognize that power.

We have already seen how important the idea of being present is in the views we have come across in this chapter. Buddhism and Taoism both encourage a focus on the present, and Marcus reminds himself that "the passing moment is all that a man can ever live or lose." For his part, Epicurus counsels, "You are not in control of tomorrow and yet you delay your [opportunity to] rejoice."[56] For Tolle, likewise, "Life is now. There was never a time when your life was *not* now, nor will there ever be."[57] And yet we fail to recognize this fact and the implications of it.

The reason for this failure, Tolle tells us, has to do with our minds, which operate in a particular way "unconsciously."

What we are unconscious of is precisely the present moment, what is happening now. How does this happen? The dynamic Tolle describes is that our minds are constantly concerned about things that involve an unawareness of the present moment. Among these things, the desire to feel important is central. We want to feel that we've accomplished significant tasks, that we are respected and loved, that we matter to others and perhaps to the universe in some larger sense. All of this leads to a constant anxiety we carry around with us. "You are in the here and now, while your mind is in the future. This creates an anxiety gap. And if you are identified with your mind and have lost touch with the power and simplicity of the Now, that anxiety gap will be your constant companion."[58]

You will recognize immediately the role Buddhism plays in Tolle's thought, a role he does not deny. Recall here that for the Buddhists, desire, which is focused on the future, is the source of suffering. Eliminate desire and you eliminate suffering. The same is true for Tolle. "True salvation is a state of freedom—from fear, from suffering, from a perceived state of lack and insufficiency and therefore from all wanting, needing, grasping, and clinging."[59] However, Tolle's approach to this has a more contemporary ring.

Recent studies of consumer behavior indicate that consumerism has an addictive aspect.[60] When a person buys something he wants, there is a temporary mild high associated with it. The high doesn't last, however, and in order to experience it again he has to buy something else. Older readers will recall former Philippine First Lady Imelda Marcos, who owned more than one thousand pairs of shoes. A more common but less extreme case occurs in many homes each December. We all know how much kids enjoy getting new toys for Christmas— the excitement that comes with tearing off the wrapping, opening the box, and seeing something new there to be enjoyed. And we all know the irritability or ennui that descends when that initial excitement wears off. Inasmuch as a person identifies himself with consumerism, he, like an addict, experiences stretches of dissatisfaction punctuated by small moments of joy. To put the matter in Tolle's terms, someone like that lives with a "perceived state of lack and insufficiency."

What goes for consumerism, though, goes for many other things. When I get recognition for a philosophical accomplishment, I often feel a sense of reward and satisfaction. That sense soon fades, and I find myself wanting to do something to gain it again. If I give in to this feeling, then my sense of who I am or what I am worth comes from outside me. It is a desire for something to be granted to me in the future that will make me feel good or worthy or whole or sufficient.

And what holds for consumerism and the desire for recognition holds for other things as well: the need to accomplish, the desire to be loved, the will to win, the ambition to be promoted at the workplace—indeed, most of the motivations we experience in our daily lives. This is precisely what Tolle calls living unconsciously, and it comes from what he calls the mind—that is, the cognitive focus on the future and what it can bring. It creates a false self, a self layered over the true self, one that is eternally restless, anxious, and unsatisfied.

What is it to live consciously, then, and what is the true self? To live consciously, Tolle says, is to be aware of the moment. It is to inhabit the present entirely, to give one's attention over to what is happening now. And the true self is the self that, in opposition to the restless and seeking self, lives consciously in that moment, accepting what is rather than seeking something else. Tolle argues that if we inhabit the current moment rather than worrying about what might or might not happen, we will realize that there is nothing we cannot accept. "Your life situation [i.e., your life as you conceive it through your false self] may be full of problems—most life situations are—but find out if you have any problem at this moment. Not tomorrow or in ten minutes, but now. Do you have a problem now?"[61] The answer, he thinks, is invariably no. That is the power of now.

There are various ways of learning to inhabit the now, many of which are linked to exercises associated with Buddhism: meditation, focus on breathing, attention to what one is thinking, attention focused on the body. All of these are ways for you to bring yourself back to the present moment. They move you away from your mind, from your concerns with what might or will happen to what is currently happening, to where you are at present. To focus on your thoughts, for example, is not to think those thoughts but to recognize the thoughts you are currently having, to distance yourself from them and see them just as thoughts you happen to be having at the moment. As you distance yourself from those thoughts—become conscious of them in Tolle's sense—their subject matter becomes less urgent. Instead, you see them for what they are: thoughts that are occurring at the moment, thoughts that can be accepted without your having to solve whatever puzzle they put in front of you.

This does not mean that you cannot have projects of any kind that extend into the future. You can embrace your projects. The difference between the true self and the false self is not that the latter has projects while the former does not. Instead, it is that the false self worries about the success or failure of those projects, while the true self is simply involved in them for what they are at the moment. This includes projects of concern to others. In fact, Tolle argues, only when a person fully inhabits the now can he be truly compassionate toward others. This is because he is no longer worried about what impression he is making or whether he will be successful in helping the other or whether he should be doing something else instead. He will be entirely given over to being with the other person at that moment.

It is not surprising then that, like the proponents of other views, Tolle believes that death should hold no fear for us. After all, death is in the future, it is not in the now. Tolle might well echo Epicurus's view that where we are, death is not, and add that if we focus entirely on where we are, then we need not worry about death. He tells us that "when a loved one has just died, or you feel your own death approaching, you cannot be happy. It is impossible. But you can be at peace. There may be sadness and tears, but provided that you have relinquished resistance, underneath the sadness you will feel a deep serenity, a stillness, a sacred presence."[62] To put the point another way, when you inhabit the now, even in the face of the death of another or your own imminent death, you remain conscious of your reactions as nothing more than reactions, such that they lose their grip. You can let them go.

Tolle's view, as he himself emphasizes, is an invulnerabilist one. It allows, as we have just seen, for a measure of sadness—or at least a lack of happiness—but not for any type of deep suffering. "Presence removes time. Without time, no suffering, no negativity, can survive."[63] To be fully in the present, to surrender yourself to what is (even if you are involved in a project of trying to change your current situation or that of others), is to end suffering, because suffering comes not from what is but from what might or might not be. This does not mean that we cannot undergo any pain at all (although Tolle does sometimes make claims about the extra physical health that arises from being fully present). If we stub our toes or have kidney stones, we will feel pain. But the difference between pain or sadness on the one hand and suffering on the other is that the former allow for a "deep serenity" beneath them, a peacefulness that enables us to accept them for what they are. By contrast, suffering is a refusal to accept, a need for something to be other than what it is.

This deep serenity, like nirvana, or the refusal to be caught up in the snares of language, or the elimination of passions, or (perhaps) the embrace of simple pleasures, renders us immune to the suffering we often associate with the failure of important projects or other life frustrations, the deaths of loved ones or our own inescapable death, the injustice we see around us or the vicarious hurt we feel from natural evils like earthquakes and disease that are the lot of so many. It doesn't, nor do the other views we have canvassed, make us cold or uncompassionate or uncaring. In fact, as these views have emphasized, it instead may allow us to be more fully engaged with those who suffer. However, what the views of Tolle, Buddhism, Taoism, Stoicism, and (again, perhaps) Epicurus seek to accomplish is to render whatever happens to us something that ultimately cannot shake us, cannot make us vulnerable in any deep way that would disturb the essential peace they offer.

The question we must turn to now, one that will occupy us for the rest of the book, is not whether this is possible. Perhaps it is. I, for one, have no reason to doubt that there are people who can achieve this kind of invulnerability. Instead, the question that will occupy us is whether most of us would really want it.

*

There is something compelling, in fact even beautiful, in these philosophical views. The vision they offer of how to live a life of equanimity, indeed serenity, cannot but be attractive for most of us at certain points. The reason I decided to wrestle with them in this book is that I found myself returning to them, thinking about them, considering the role they might play in steadying my own periodically fraught existence. This is especially true, in my case, of Taoism. The person who became my spiritual guide during my adolescence is a Taoist, and the advice he gave me that prevented me from being too buffeted about by my emotions—particularly the dark ones, which were often in the foreground—frequently came from his understanding of Chuang Tzu's thought, occasionally peppered with similar insights from Buddhism. Later, in my immersion in Western philosophy, I came across Stoicism and Epicurus, and while I found the latter more plausible than the former, I often taught and read Marcus's *Meditations* with an interest that was more than academic curiosity.

There is much, I am still convinced, to be gained by reading, thinking about, and adopting many aspects of these views. In the final chapter, I will return to what I take to be important lessons and helpful spiritual exercises they offer us. Nevertheless, the invulnerabilism they ultimately embrace is, to my mind, too disengaged emotionally from the world for any of them to be a philosophical view that I could allow to guide my own life. I believe I am not alone in this. Most of us, I suspect, would reject the invulnerabilism common to these views in favor of a less serene existence and would be willing to pay the price associated with that loss of serenity. In fact, the point might be put in a stronger way: most of us simply could not and would not want to see ourselves living the invulnerabilism commended by these views.

If this is true, there is an important philosophical task to which we must turn. We must seek to articulate the kind of vulnerability that would be more attractive to us than invulnerability, the kind of life that most of us would be willing to ratify—a life that takes on the lessons of these views but rejects their invulnerabilism. That will be the task of the final chapter, although chapter 4 will lay the groundwork for it. Before that, however, we need to reflect on the reasons for rejecting invulnerabilism. Why is it, we might ask, that invulnerabilism seems not simply beyond the ability but beyond the desire of so many of us? I think there are four reasons for this, reasons concerning politics, death, failure, and loss. I will approach them in this order, although, as we will see, they are related and sometimes refer to one another. The reason for the order I have chosen is that, to my mind, each one is increasingly difficult for invulnerabilism to deal with. That is, each distances us from invulnerabilism in a way that is increasingly difficult for invulnerabilism to accommodate on its own terms.

Before turning to this task, however, let me dispose of one common criticism of invulnerabilist doctrines. I often hear it from my undergraduate students when I discuss one or another of these doctrines. If the goal is to end suffering, they ask, why not just commit suicide? After all, wouldn't suicide dispose of suffering quickly and without all the bother of meditation and self-transformation? The response to this is that suicide is not a way to overcome desire or attachment but instead a succumbing to them. While it is true that suicide would end suffering, it would end it not by rising above its causes but rather by allowing oneself to be overwhelmed by them. What invulnerabilism commends to us is not giving in to our desires but the opposite: to end their grip on us. If suicide, in its way, ends the grip of our desires on us by ending our lives, it does so by falling headlong into that grip. In that way suicide runs contrary to the orientation of the various invulnerabilist doctrines we are treating here.

Let us turn then to the first reason for rejecting invulnerabilism. It is no secret that our world is filled with injustice. In many parts of the world, the politics of injustice is pervasive. Autocracy, racism, oppression, misogyny, homophobia, exploitation, and domination are daily fare in many parts of the planet and are common to one degree or another in all. The question that arises is one of how invulnerabilist doctrines would have us face them. My early concern with these doctrines was that they would not have us face them at all. Their focus seemed to me to be on changing oneself rather than the world. In every case, the approach favored by these views struck me as, Don't worry about the world, worry about yourself. This, it seemed to me, was exactly the wrong approach to life in a world as soaked in injustice as our world is. In fact, although I gained most of the credits for a doctorate in psychology—I was hoping to be a therapist—I left the field precisely because of the pervasiveness of that attitude. Psychology as a therapeutic field appeared to me then—and, for the most part, continues to appear to me—to commend leaving the world as it is and changing oneself to fit more smoothly into its flow.[64] With the current domination of psychiatric drugs, this orientation is even more pronounced.

However, over the years I began to see that invulnerabilist doctrines are more nuanced than the psychology I left behind. It would be a mistake to say that they are unconcerned with justice. Buddhism and Stoicism in particular are insistent in their concern for making a more just world—Buddhism through the actions of the bodhisattva and Stoicism through its focus on acting rationally. We have seen this in our discussion. There is no reason to believe that Taoism or the thought of Epicurus or Tolle would be any more stinting in their interest in the welfare of others. To be sure, none of these doctrines offers a comprehensive view of justice or a program for how we should act to promote it. That is not their task. However, there is nothing in them that would counsel leaving the world as it is in favor of gaining personal serenity.

In fact, as we have seen, in one way these doctrines might make it *easier* for someone to engage in projects of justice. If someone is comfortable with her own existence, she might be more likely to be attuned to the suffering of others, since she is untroubled in her own life. We know that when we suffer it is often difficult to see outside of it to the worries, legitimate though they may be, of others. We are caught up in our own troubles. Perhaps, an invulnerabilist might argue, if we can get past our own suffering we would be more open to that of others and therefore better positioned to work on behalf of justice than someone who has not achieved invulnerability— or at least a good measure of it.

I believe this response is relevant and in some ways compelling. It is difficult to be attuned to the suffering of others and to injustice in general when I am caught up in personal difficulty. And someone who is at peace with herself is not going to be burdened with this. In short, my earlier criticism of these doctrines was off the mark. However, I don't think it was entirely misplaced, and this for two reasons. First, there remains, in these views, what we might call an "inward" orientation. They privilege a concern with oneself that can easily lead away from political concerns toward more personal ones. When someone is seeking to maintain her own equanimity, it can become imperative to arrange her involvements so that her equanimity is not disturbed. Political involvement, by contrast, often involves placing oneself in situations of stress and conflict. So someone who is trying to be at peace might well be led away from rather than toward projects of justice.

To be fair, this is not an implication of the views themselves but rather a concern with how they might be taken up. However, given that people who are drawn to these views (among whom I count myself) are often looking for some kind of peace, it is an outcome that would not be surprising among many who utilize them.

The second reason for wariness about the compatibility of living invulnerably and promoting justice is complementary to the first. The concern for justice often arises not out of a sense of serenity or equanimity but precisely from its opposite, a distress about the state of the world. People are disturbed by the injustices they see in the world and feel that they cannot be entirely comfortable with themselves unless they are doing something to mitigate or confront those injustices. I have been involved in many political struggles for justice; my experience is that most of the people in them are motivated not through an equanimity that they seek to bring to others but rather through an ongoing sense that they will not and ought not find any serenity until the injustices they confront are overcome.

An adherent of invulnerabilism might complain here that none of this really weakens the concern for justice in invulnerabilist doctrines. The reason so many people are motivated by disturbance rather than through equanimity, it might be said, is that so few people have actually achieved the equanimity commended by these doctrines. The problem lies not in the doctrines themselves but in the rarity with which they are fully taken up.

This response seems to me to miss two important points. The first, which we will consider more fully in the final chapter, is that invulnerabilist doctrines narrow the range of human emotion and reaction. If they were taken up by everyone, they would eliminate much of the diversity of human living that is an enlivening aspect of our world. Second, by withdrawing distress as a motive to confront injustice, invulnerabilism eliminates one currently important source of political action. This runs the risk of decreasing the level of political involvement in struggles against injustice, since distress is perhaps the dominant source of such action. Here again, the invulnerabilist might reply that the reason this source is dominant is that there are so few invulnerabilists out there. This is certainly true. However, unless we are confident of a mass conversion to invulnerabilism followed by a turn to political action motivated through equanimity, then we should recognize the danger of removing the main catalyst of current struggles against injustice.

The second reason for resistance to invulnerabilism concerns its relation to death. Invulnerabilism counsels comfort with the fact of mortality for a variety of reasons. For traditional Buddhism, this is because people will be reborn until they reach nirvana. For Taoism it is that we will merge with the earth and become something else or part of something else. Stoicism insists on the rationality of the universe that makes us mortal, while Epicurus points out that where death is, we are not. Tolle, in his turn, reminds us that living in the present will turn us away from future worries and concerns. There is nothing wrong with these counsels as far as they go. The problem is that, in commending a particular relation to death, they leave out other equally valid relationships to one's death that might be lived.

The poet Dylan Thomas is famous for insisting that we "do not go gently into that good night" but instead "rage, rage against the dying of the light." Should we reject this approach as being inappropriate? For my own part, I would like to feel as though I could face imminent death with more equanimity and less rage. At the same time, I can admire the intensity coiled in Thomas's poem. It is not difficult to imagine someone so burning with energy, even up to her old age, that death becomes a matter for rejection rather than embrace or resignation. For this person, no matter how much living she has done, there is more remaining. She is not ready to go, not because she has not yet lived, not because she has regrets (perhaps there is nothing she has done that she would not have), but because she can still see so much that she has not yet done. The pull of what is left to do renders it impossible for her to go gently into that good night, no matter how full her life has been.

The idea here is not that she has had a better life than the rest of us. Nor is it that her raging against the dying of the light is preferable to the more peaceful relation to death proffered by the invulnerabilists. At least on this score, I find my own orientation aligned with invulnerabilism. Rather, we ought to allow that there are different relations a person may take to her own death, and which is better—if any—may well depend on the life she has lived. It may be faced with a certain serenity, perhaps tinged with sadness that one is at the end of a worthy journey. However, what parades as serenity might also be resignation, perhaps tinged not with sadness but with regret. It may be that the person who rages against her death does so because she has never stopped living. She has not, like many of us, allowed old age to be an excuse raised against embarking on new projects or throwing herself into uncomfortable situations. In short, it is not what invulnerabilism commends in regard to death that I want to challenge, but rather what it rejects in that commendation.

Someone might argue here on behalf of invulnerabilism that raging against the dying of the light is not a sign of a life lived intensely but rather of a failure to come to terms with the fact that one is dying. It must necessarily involve regret, since the person herself believes she has left much undone. This would not be entirely false. However, it is only a half-truth. To this person, it is certainly regrettable that she has not been allotted the time to do more, and there are probably particular activities she has not engaged in that leave her with a sense of loss at her impending end. On the other hand, this need not be due to any failure on her part to have done what she ought to have done or wanted to do. It need not be a sense of emptiness but instead one of being overfilled with intellectual curiosity or a passion for justice yet unmet or sheer spontaneity that drive her to press against the death that is coming. If some of us are too ready to feel that her desire to live more in the face of death is a sign of having not lived well, perhaps it may be our own inability to take up life with her intensity that is speaking rather than any wisdom about mortality.

The third reason one might reject invulnerabilism has to do with our relation to failure, particularly the failure of important projects. Invulnerabilism counsels us not to feel regret or remorse at failed projects. It is a tenet of invulnerabilism that neither past nor future exist, only the present; it is pointless to focus emotionally on anything else, particularly anything one cannot change. As we have seen, this does not preclude making plans for the future or seeking to assist others. What it does preclude is any attachment to what happens as a result of our plans and actions. If the future does not yet exist for invulnerabilism, it at least is a horizon toward which we can move. The past is entirely inert. There is no reason to dwell on what has occurred, since it cannot be altered.

For many of us, this advice, although it has a certain logic, rings false. To be sure, it is often easy to focus on the past in unhelpful ways. And indeed it is true that we cannot change what has happened. Furthermore, a healthy relation to the past would not simply involve regret or remorse but also a willingness to draw lessons for the future, a willingness that can be allowed by invulnerabilism. But is there really no place for looking back with disappointment, sorrow, repentance, or perhaps even bitterness?

The philosopher Robert Adams, in an essay on what makes life meaningful, recalls the life of the German officer Claus von Stauffenberg. Stauffenberg fought on the German side during World War II, although he hated the Nazi regime. Along with several others, he sought to save Germany from Hitler's rule, and in the summer of 1944 led the famous Operation Valkyrie, a failed attempt to assassinate Hitler by planting a bomb in his headquarters. The bomb did detonate, but Hitler was not killed. Afterward, Stauffenberg was shot by the Nazi regime. Adams writes, "Not much is known about how Stauffenberg *felt* when he was finally compelled to recognize, late in the evening of July 20th, that his conspiracy to overthrow Nazism had failed. Someone he spoke to then thought he looked 'indescribably sad.'"[65]

Let's imagine Stauffenberg looking back at his actions before being executed. He had tried to save Germany from the most evil ruler of modern times and had failed. Germany was disgraced and Hitler's cruelty would continue, even if for not much longer. Should we follow the invulnerabilists in thinking that he should not regret or even be disappointed in his failure? He needn't have blamed himself. He could have considered his actions and realized that there was nothing else he could have done. Given the events as they unfolded, it seems that Stauffenberg was unlucky in a way he couldn't have helped. Would this make it unreasonable for him to be despondent that he did not succeed in the assassination?

We can go further. Let's imagine him looking back on his actions and saying to himself, "Well, that didn't work out. However, that is the past and I can only live in the now." What would be our reaction to that? We might wonder how much he actually cared about achieving his goal. It would seem strange to most of us if Stauffenberg could pull himself away emotionally from a failed attempt to rescue his country from the devastation it was undergoing. It would be difficult to square such an attitude with the depth of caring necessary for him to risk the plan in the first place. And yet that is what the invulnerabilist would counsel him to feel. Of course it is correct that Stauffenberg could not change the past. He could not go back and try again. However, given the stakes, there is something odd about taking that fact to be the salient one rather than the fact of the failure itself. It is that latter fact and the disappointment it would elicit that most of us would think of as occupying his mind in the hours before his execution.

I don't want to argue that it would be impossible for him to be invested in the assassination attempt and then turn his mind to the present moment after its failure. There might be Stoics, Buddhists, and others who could do so. And I don't even want to claim that it is better that he should be disappointed or frustrated with his failure. The fact that many of us would find it odd if he weren't disappointed does not show that he should have been or that it would be inappropriate if he weren't. After all, we could imagine his having the reaction that the past is just the past and, when questioned about this, replying, "I'm a Stoic and have trained myself to live in this way." Alternatively, he might say to himself that he did his best and that's all he could do and that the rest was simply not up to him. I, for one, could accept that as a reasonable explanation for what would strike me initially as an odd reaction.

My claim is more modest: there is nothing wrong or untoward in the disappointment. Finding it appropriate that he focused on the failure rather than that failure's being in the past does not seem unwarranted. However, according to invulnerabilism it would be. It would be a failure to let go of his desire or an investment of passion or a dwelling on the past instead of the present or some such. For many of us, however, probably most, disappointment or regret would be a reaction we would relate to and, more important, that *we would want to relate to*. There seems to be nothing amiss about Stauffenberg's being despondent when his attempt to save Germany lay in ruins and he was facing execution. Put another way, while the invulnerabilist would not be mistaken in her account of the facts, and would not be wrong to say that someone could react to these in an invulnerabilist fashion, many of us would not be interested in such a reaction and would find it odd if Stauffenberg exhibited it.

It might be argued here that I have skewed things with my example. It is so extreme that it seems to force us away from invulnerabilism. I have two responses to this argument. First, invulnerabilism itself is forced to respond in this way to the example in its extremity. The problem, if there is one, does not belong to the example but instead to the reaction invulnerabilism would endorse. Second, and more important, we do not need to go to such extremity in order to see the appropriateness of disappointment, regret, despondency, or remorse over a failed project. While it may be true that many of us are too readily distressed about failures that in the larger scheme of things don't really matter, there are plenty of projects whose failure it would be perfectly appropriate to react to with one or another expression of backward-looking misgiving. A person whose child turned out to be a drug addict or to have a miserable life, someone who dedicates her own life to a project of social justice that never succeeds or that she realizes later she was on the wrong side of, a corporate executive who decides near retirement that she would rather have been a social worker or a teacher, an athlete who becomes injured and lives in pain wondering whether she would have had a better existence if she had not been an athlete, a donor who gives a lot of money to a charity that turns out to be a scam, someone who works for a politician whose real commitments turn out to be different from her stated ones, even a person who spends several years working to save a local school or factory that eventually closes: all of these failures in their different ways seem to allow for, even if they don't demand, disappointment, regret, or even in some cases anguish. Such a reaction would not just be a display of understandable human weakness. It would be a display of human caring. For most of us, invulnerabilists notwithstanding, what it means to care requires vulnerability in the face of failure.

We have seen three reasons to reject invulnerabilism, each with increasing strength, from concerns about political inertia to the facing of death to reactions to failure. The fourth reason harks back to Anaxagoras's own reaction to news of his son's death: he always knew his son was a mortal. If we are to be invulnerabilists, then what happens in the world outside of us cannot or at least should not affect us. We must be immune to its assaults. There are few greater assaults than the loss of a loved one: a spouse, a close friend, or especially a child. However, invulnerabilism counsels us to recognize the loss as simply one that has occurred in the past. It need not have bearing on the present.

Grieving, for the invulnerabilist, is a failure to understand this. We can see this in different ways in the five views we have canvassed. For traditional Buddhism, reincarnation, since it denies the existence of death for those of us who have not reached nirvana, would not count the loss of a loved one as a loss. It would instead be a transformation from one life form to another. Even without the doctrines of reincarnation and karma, however, Buddhism would still counsel against grieving, since grieving desires that the loved one still be alive. This desire need not be for one's own sake. I can desire that my friend or lover have more time to enjoy her own life rather than to bring joy to mine. Since that remains a desire, it would violate the Four Noble Truths central to Buddhist doctrine.

The story of Masters Li and Lai related by Chuang Tzu display Taoism's attitude toward loss. Master Li brushes aside the concerns of the Lai family as their not understanding that Master Lai's death will simply return him to the One from which he arose and allow him to assume other life forms, perhaps a rat's liver or a bug's arm. Equally, we have seen Epictetus recommend preparation for the deaths of one's spouse and children so that their deaths, if they precede one's own, will not affect one.[66] As the philosopher John Cooper says of the Stoics, "Stoic virtuous people, whatever they do feel, do not feel [grief] at all—even mildly, or moderately, or with reservations."[67] In Tolle's case, living entirely in the present precludes concern with what has happened. If a death has happened to someone we know, it has happened in the past and therefore cannot inform our attitude toward the present moment.

As always, Epicurus's view on this matter is a bit more complicated. On the one hand, he commends simple pleasures that allow us a measure of peace with the world. Moreover, his fourfold view that we should not fear God, recognize that death is not a problem, know that good is easily obtainable and evil easily bearable would lead us to think that grieving is a mistake. There is no need to grieve lost loved ones for our own sake, since grief will not bring us pleasure and their loss is easily bearable. And there is no need to grieve the loss for the sake of the loved ones, since they are not there any longer and so it is no loss for them. On the other hand, we have seen that for Epicurus friendship is one of the great goods among the simple pleasures. If this is so, then it would seem that the loss of a friend is the subtraction of a necessary pleasure for myself even if it is not for the friend. This would lead us toward a view of Epicurus as more nearly open to grief than the other, more committed invulnerabilist views.

Why is the rejection of grief common to these views? What is wrong with it? Why would any of us reject grief, and would we be justified in doing so? For most of us, it is difficult to square caring deeply for others with not being moved by their loss. Grief is both for our sake and for the sake of the one lost. From our side, those we care about are woven into our lives. They are central to what make our lives meaningful to us, a fact that Epicurus recognized—although we need not cast this meaningfulness in the language of pleasure that he uses. As temporal creatures—creatures of the past and the future and not merely the present—we see who we have been and who we would like to become not merely in terms of our individual lives but, just as important, in terms of our relationships with others. Who I have been is to a great degree who I have been with those I care about. To lose someone I care about, then, is to lose part of myself, part of who I have been and who I can be in the future. It is to have a piece of what makes my life meaningful shorn away from me.

This does not mean that I cannot recover or that I cannot develop closeness with another. But there is no substitutability here. If I develop new relationships with others, this will result in a different type of meaningfulness for my own life than the type I had with the person with whom I previously shared it. This would be so even if the new relationship mirrored the old one. For it is not only the likeness of the person to the lost one that matters. It is the fact that the lost one is the particular person she is—that person with whom I shared that portion of my life—that has animated it so and whose loss therefore cannot be redeemed.[68]

From the side of the person who is lost, I grieve because he will no longer have the joys of living before him. For most people, being alive is worth the difficulties it involves. That is why so few of us consider suicide very seriously or for very long. The loss of a life, even if the person is no longer there to experience the loss, is a loss of what would have been had he not died. Our grief at the death of someone about whom we care marks a recognition of that loss. It is difficult to see how someone could recognize that loss on the one hand and not *feel* it on the other.

Although it may be possible to care about another for his own sake and yet entirely let him go on the other, this seems beyond the ability of most of us. More deeply, though, I think it is beyond the desire of most of us. If I care about someone for his own sake, while I do not desire the grief itself, I would not desire not to grieve. Grief seems a proper recognition of a loss that has taken place both for me and for the person who was there. It is a melancholy for the meaning that has been leaked away from me and a respect for the one who is no longer with me.

Invulnerabilism's inability to recognize the role of grieving is, to my mind, the most important reason to reject it as an approach to living. Combined with its refusal to countenance feelings of failure, its lack of recognition of other attitudes toward death as being equally as valid as serenity, and its potential political shortcomings, invulnerabilism, for all of its insights, seems to counsel a way of living that would not be attractive for most of us. However, on the other hand, invulnerabilist views have provided us with numerous insights that cannot be forgotten even if we ultimately jettison the invulnerabilism defended by these views. This leaves us with a question, then. How can we take up the insights of invulnerabilism while still allowing ourselves a fragility that we would not want to forsake? How might we live vulnerably and yet with a certain sense of balance? I begin to open that issue in the following chapter, and in the final chapter I attempt to address it directly.

FROM AFFIRMATION TO ACCEPTANCE

Sometimes in philosophy we can gain perspective by wrestling with a single example. Seeing how someone views this example, engaging with their view, and drawing our own conclusions allows us to open perspectives that might otherwise be closed to us. In most of this chapter we will be doing precisely that. The example we will wrestle with is one we've seen in passing already: the bourgeois professor mentioned in the second chapter. Offered by the philosopher R. Jay Wallace, this example, to his mind, points in a direction almost opposite of that of invulnerabilism. It points to a necessary pessimism about our lives.

If we reflect on Wallace's example, and the perspective through which Wallace sees it, I believe we can move past both the pessimism of his view and the invulnerabilism of the last chapter toward a more balanced and more attractive way of thinking about our relation to suffering. That way can be crystallized in a single word: *acceptance*. But to see what acceptance is in this particular sense requires us to frame an entire perspective, one that I think will feel at once familiar and novel. We will slowly work our way to that perspective in this chapter and then unfold it in the next.

For Wallace, there are aspects of our lives that we cannot help affirming but that we know we should reject. In *The View from Here: On Affirmation, Attachment, and the Limits of Regret*, Wallace argues for what he calls a "modest nihilism."[1] This nihilism stems from the fact that we—or at least many of us—live in ways that force us to affirm aspects of our lives that we know to be morally compromised. The reason for this, broadly speaking, is that in becoming the particular people we are in the ways that we value most, we do so on the basis of a past that is morally flawed, often deeply so.

We should clarify for ourselves what Wallace means by *affirmation*. He posits what he calls an "affirmation dynamic" that characterizes our relation to important (or, as we will see, perhaps all) aspects of our past. He writes, in a passage that perhaps illustrates why more people don't read philosophy, "If we are attached to an individual or a project, then we will typically affirm the direct objects of our affirmation in a distinctively unconditional way; this in turn commits us to affirming their necessary constitutive and historical and normative conditions in a way that is similarly unconditional, and precludes our regretting that those conditions obtained. We might refer to this as the dynamic of unconditional affirmation (or the 'affirmation dynamic' in short)."[2]

What does he mean here? The affirmation dynamic arises in regard to something that is important to us, be it a person, an object, or a personal commitment. In affirming the existence of that person, object, or personal commitment, we cannot simply affirm its existence separate from everything else that has happened to us or that we have done. We must also affirm whatever gave rise to that existence. In a simple case, if I care for my partner, I must affirm the conditions that gave rise to her, for instance her parents, her background, aspects of her particular history, and so on. I must affirm these things because, had they been different, she would not even be here, or at least not be the person she is, the person I have come to care about.

What is it to affirm something in this way? Wallace is clear that this does not require that we feel good about everything we affirm. We might feel bad about some aspects of a past that gave rise to a worthy present. However, if we are to exhibit unconditional affirmation, what we cannot do is wish, ultimately, that things had been otherwise. We cannot have what Wallace calls "all-in regret." That is, we might wish that what led to the thing we affirm had come about otherwise, but we can't ultimately reject the way it came about if we really do affirm that thing.

We can see this affirmation dynamic at work in different aspects of our lives. When I got my position teaching at a university, there were many others who applied for the position. I wish they hadn't had to undergo the rejection they did in order for me to get the position. But, had things unfolded differently, I wouldn't have gotten the position myself. To affirm my having this position requires that I not have "all-in regret" for how my getting this position came about. There are athletes who come to prominence because people who were ahead of them in the roster sustained injury. A famous case is that of the New England Patriots quarterback Tom Brady, who took over the position of starting quarterback when Drew Bledsoe was injured. Given the subsequent trajectory of his career, it might be difficult for Brady to regret Bledsoe's injury, even if he would have preferred to get the starting job some other way.

The affirmation dynamic does not preclude personal discomfort or a regret that things came about in the way that they did. I might prefer that the past situation did not have to be the way it was in order for things to be the way they currently are. However, given that they are the way they currently are, and given that the way they came to be the way they currently are is on the basis of the particular past that led them here, I cannot ultimately regret that past having happened. I might wish for a better past, but only if it would have led to this particular present, for instance the present that includes the existence of my partner or the present for Tom Brady of being the starting quarterback for his football team. One cannot just wish for a better past independent of the things one affirms. In fact, to wish for it is no real wish at all, since any given present is the result of a particular past. Thus the affirmation dynamic commits one to endorsing the past in a way that precludes all-in regret.

In the second chapter, we saw the affirmation dynamic at work in the examples of the young mother, the imagined Paul Gauguin, and the bourgeois professor. It is this last example that I want to focus on. Wallace calls it the "bourgeois predicament." His general characterization of it is this: "Our ground projects are the basis of our affirmative attitude toward the lives that we lead. But their bourgeois character means that those projects implicate us in social and economic disparities that we cannot possibly endorse (not at any rate if we are reasonable and thoughtful)."[3] The "ground projects" in question here (a term he borrows from Bernard Williams and that we have already seen) are the fundamental projects that lend our lives meaning, the projects we have here called our central projects. They are those projects that make our lives feel worthwhile to ourselves, whether they are our love relationships, our careers, our friendships, our commitment to social justice projects, some combination of these, or something else altogether.

In the case of the bourgeois predicament, the problem at issue is not a decision that one has made previously, as with the young mother or the imagined Gauguin. Instead, it is the set of social, political, and economic arrangements that allow some of us to benefit at the expense of others. It is the set of circumstances we find ourselves in, and the way they came about without our participation, without our molding them, that causes the difficulty.

As a specific case of the bourgeois predicament, Wallace asks us to imagine a life, presumably much like his own or those of some of his readers, of a philosophy professor at a good university. As we know, universities were often built on the backs of exploited labor, and even slave labor. They are sustained through corporate investments that themselves may be exploitative as well as through underpaid labor at the university (janitors, secretaries, and the like). Moreover, universities often act as conduits either through research or through social connections to sustain the very inegalitarian conditions that gave rise and sustenance to them. Thus, to be a professor of philosophy at such a university is to be implicated in "social and economic disparities that we cannot possibly endorse."

This is not to deny that there is value to the profession of philosophy. As there is value for the child of the young mother and value in Gauguin's painting, so there is value in philosophy: in teaching it, in writing about it, and in the very act of philosophical reflection. However, the structure of academic philosophy is sustained by conditions that, Wallace believes, cannot withstand moral assessment. Academic philosophy cannot be what it is without having relied on and continuing to rely on oppressive social, political, and economic conditions. Moreover, inasmuch as being an academic philosopher is a ground project, a project that makes our living worthwhile—and for many of us it is—the situation we find ourselves in is that an important aspect of what gives our lives meaning stems from conditions that are morally repugnant.

Wallace considers three ways of dealing with the bourgeois predicament and finds them all wanting. There is first the strategy of denial: acting as though the predicament isn't actually a problem. This is unacceptable for obvious reasons: willful moral blindness is hardly to be commended as a way of going about one's life. Second, there is the strategy of withdrawal. Instead of denying that the problem exists, we remove ourselves from the specific social conditions that give rise to these problems. This, however, is impossible for most of us. We are woven into the fabric of our society, and thus its oppressions. As long as we remain socially engaged, we simply cannot withdraw. Third, there is the strategy of redemption. This involves seeking to struggle against the current conditions that contribute to the predicament. Wallace's argument against this strategy has two parts. On the one hand, he argues that in order to engage in such struggle one has to rely on the resources—material resources, leisure time—that are partly constitutive of the very predicament itself. On the other hand, inasmuch as one identifies with the struggle against oppression, one's life projects become defined by what one is against, thus reinforcing the role of oppression as a matter of one's ground projects. Let us look briefly at each in turn.

Wallace argues, "Those who seek to escape from their implication in impersonally lamentable conditions by dedicating themselves to improving those conditions rely on the very thing that they are trying to escape. It is only those who stand in a privileged position in the distribution of resources who have the luxury of giving meaning to their lives through the project of helping to address the plight of the least advantaged members of our social world."[4] It is because I, as a professor of philosophy, am not struggling to make ends meet, am not working extra hours to feed my family, and am not too tired at the end of the day to engage in extracurricular activities, that I can engage in a project of redemption. And it is only because I benefit from those "impersonally lamentable conditions" that I am in a position to do this.

The other problem lies in my identification with the conditions against which I am seeking to redeem myself. "Dedicating one's life to the project of combating inequality and deprivation has the perverse effect that one comes to define oneself primarily in terms of the lamentable conditions that one sets oneself against."[5] Moreover, if this becomes a ground project, then this definition threatens to withdraw deep meaning from one's life should the inequality and deprivation be ameliorated. "People whose defining project is that of combating global inequality and deprivation could not retain that source of meaning in a counterfactual situation in which those conditions had been altogether eliminated."[6] Ironically, to be successful in the struggle against inequality and oppression would not lend meaning to one's life but would instead be the source of its disappearance.

One can see why Wallace characterizes his position as one of "modest nihilism." We who are in privileged positions in the world, as well as those who make decisions similar or analogous to those made by the young mother or the imagined Gauguin, find ourselves having to affirm conditions that are not morally acceptable, even to us. We might refuse to look at this dilemma; however, that does not make it go away. We are, many of us, implicated in situations in which we find ourselves endorsing what we know we should condemn in order for our lives to have the meaning they do.

I believe that Wallace's view of the bourgeois predicament is mistaken, and on two levels. First, his criticism of the strategy of redemption seems to me to be misguided. Second, and more deeply, there is an important disanalogy between the situations of the young mother and the imagined Gauguin on the one hand and the bourgeois predicament on the other. This second matter will lead us into a normative arena that Wallace does not consider, that of acceptance as opposed to affirmation. And that, in turn, can lead us to a different attitude toward some of the vexed areas of our life. However, before we turn there, let us linger briefly over the first problem.

The strategy of redemption, according to Wallace, requires both that we make use of our privileged status to struggle against inequality and deprivation and that we identify with what we are opposing, or rather with our opposition. We can, however, accept both of these claims without having to embrace the idea that they imply some sort of predicament. Regarding the first, let's suppose, for instance, that I, as a philosophy professor, use some of my salary and my free time to contribute money and volunteer work to a unionization effort that, if successful, will change the salaries and working conditions of the university's janitors. And let's suppose further that this change, if successful, will entail changes to my own working conditions. Universities are often financially strapped, after all. So if the janitors' salaries go up, mine will have to go down. Furthermore, if they are offered more free time, for instance, this will result in my having to take on some tasks that are currently theirs. I might, for instance, find myself having to sort through my own garbage in order to separate the recyclables from the nonrecyclables. In addition, I might have to take each to their proper receptacles. Perhaps our offices won't be cleaned as often, and so if I want a cleaner office I will have to bring some cleaning products and do it myself. (In case this seems unrealistic, my own university has, as a cost-cutting measure, instituted these changes. They have not, however, been accompanied by salary raises or increased free time for the janitorial staff.)

The result of all this will be a fairer distribution of salary and labor. But we can imagine further changes. Let's suppose that among those will be free university classes for janitors, to be taught by faculty on a rotating basis. If we like, we can imagine that these classes, in order to ensure that they don't constitute a financial burden on the university, are taught on a volunteer basis. I suspect that such an arrangement, although it would not draw universal participation among faculty, would be workable. Enough faculty are likely to volunteer for such a program to make it viable. Among the many benefits of such a program would be that it would reduce the educational distance between the faculty and the janitors alongside the earlier improvements to salary and free time.

All of this, we are imagining, comes about in small part through the financial contributions and time I (and others) dedicate to a unionization campaign. In this case, I have used my privileged status in a strategy of redemption. Why would that be a problem? I have used my privileged status to undermine many of those very privileges. It seems that there is no real predicament here that is impossible for me to escape. The nihilistic conclusion at which Wallace arrives is unjustified.

Here Wallace might say that I have escaped the predicament only by escaping its bourgeois character. In other words, what has allowed me to maintain my project as a philosopher are the very conditions that I am struggling against. If I am, alongside others of course, successful in struggling against those conditions, then I can no longer carry on my project in the way that I had. I will have undermined the bourgeois privilege and with it a ground project of mine.

I do not see why this is so. Certainly a high salary is not a necessary condition of being a philosopher, or any other kind of academic. In other countries, academics are often not paid as well as they are in the United States, and yet they seem to produce quality work. The only place of compromise will be in the area of leisure time. It is true that I would have less time to read and reflect under the new conditions. However, recall that, in the example, being a philosopher is a ground project. It is one of the central sources of the meaningfulness of my life. Therefore, it seems reasonable to assume that I would be willing to sacrifice some of my current leisure activities in order to make more room for philosophical work. Perhaps I won't watch those reruns of *The Wire* or will read fewer novels in the evening or will take fewer trips out of town. If philosophy is a ground project for me, none of these sacrifices will be onerous.

It seems, then, that the strategy of redemption, using my privileged status to struggle against the privilege, does not produce some sort of inescapable predicament. How about the other aspect of the problem: that I am identifying myself with what I am struggling against, or at least with the opposition itself? It reminds me of a line from the comedian Lenny Bruce, in response to the charge that he made his living from everything that was wrong or warped in society. If everything were okay, he said, he'd be on the dole, right after J. Edgar Hoover (the founder of the Federal Bureau of Investigation and at that time a publicly admired figure). Anyone who struggles to address oppression, or more widely to solve a problem, will find herself without a project—even a ground project—when that problem is solved or that issue addressed. This is simply the price one pays for successfully solving the problem in the first place. One can imagine that, once one overcomes the challenge a problem or an issue presents, there will be not only joy or relief but also a sense of letdown and, if the project is a ground project, a certain hole in one's life. But that hole is the product of accomplishment, of successfully engaging in a project, not the loss of identification with the problem itself. Otherwise put, in solving a problem generally or addressing oppression as in our example, people identify not with the problem itself but instead with the goal of solving it. And success in that goal, while perhaps leaving them temporarily at a loss for what to do next, is compensated for by having brought a project to a worthy conclusion.

Contrast the solution of a problem on the one hand with the loss of a loved one on the other. For several years in the 1980s, while I was a graduate student, I worked in the antiapartheid "divestment" movement at my university. When I wasn't studying, I was thinking about, talking to people about, and organizing for divestment, trying to come up with strategies to pressure my university into ridding its investment portfolio of stocks held in companies that did business with South Africa. In the end, our campaign was successful. This left me feeling not only relieved (it is hard to feel pure joy when the accomplishment is only a small contribution to ending an egregious wrong) and also at a bit of a loss. Of course, there are always other oppressions to fight, and I soon got involved in a couple of them. However, there was something about the antiapartheid struggle—and its victory—that remains special to me.

If, instead, the loss had been that of a loved one rather than that ground project, the situation would have been entirely different. There would have been no sense of completion, no sense of a task that had been brought successfully to a conclusion. The ground project of loving engagement would have been frustrated rather than fulfilled. In identifying with the loved one, the death would simply have cut me off from the project of cultivating our relationship. It would have undermined an aspect of the meaningfulness of my life in the ways we discussed near the end of the previous chapter. It is in that kind of loss, rather than in the solving of a problem, where identification with the project that comes to an end undermines one's sense of oneself.

It seems, then, that the strategy of redemption requires neither of the untoward features Wallace associates with it. Although someone in a bourgeois position may well have the time and resources to struggle successfully against the unequal treatment and deprivation of those who are the object of such wrongs, this does not mean that someone cannot escape the more deleterious aspects of the position she finds herself in. And in struggling against inequality and deprivation, it is not these wrongs with which she is identified, or even the opposition to them, but rather their elimination. The loss of a ground project associated with their elimination is different from the kind of loss that comes from a ground project that is stymied rather than completed.

However, there is another, deeper difficulty associated with the bourgeois predicament, one that cannot be addressed by a strategy of redemption, or by any strategy at all. The bourgeois predicament arises not only on the basis of current inequality and deprivation but also on the basis of past wrongs. And those wrongs cannot be righted. One cannot undo the various links with slavery that helped develop and sustain universities.[7] Nor can one address the exploitation that maintained them and that forms part of the basis for the structure of one's own current position. These bases of a bourgeois career are forever out of one's control.

Why might this matter? Wallace has argued that affirming one's current situation means affirming all the history that got one there. Affirming my situation as a bourgeois professor, then, commits me to affirming those past oppressions that created the conditions allowing for my position to exist. Otherwise put, inasmuch as I identify with my philosophical career as a ground project, I cannot have all-in regret for the circumstances that allow me to engage in it. This does not mean that I cannot feel bad about them. But I cannot wish them to be other than they were, since to do so would preclude me from engaging in this particular ground project.

This remains true even if I struggle to end the oppressions that helped create my situation in the ways we just discussed. Even if I reject the current conditions that sustain my bourgeois existence, the fact that I am in this position and able to engage in such *current* struggle—inasmuch as it is a ground project of mine—requires me to affirm the *past* conditions that created the possibility for this ground project.

There is more and worse to come. It is not only the particular past conditions bound up with the institutional structures in which I find myself that must be affirmed. It is instead everything that has allowed me to find myself in this position. In order for me to have been positioned to receive this professorship, I must have been educated enough to be competitive for it. So it is not only the oppressive conditions that created the current institution that must be in place but also the conditions that created the other institutions I have been associated with: my graduate school, my undergraduate university, and perhaps even my high school. And that is only the beginning. If my parents hadn't had sex at the time and place that they did, I wouldn't even be here. So I must affirm the conditions that led to their having sex, which means I must affirm the conditions under which they met. In my own case, my father went to officer's training school during World War II and later went to graduate school, which led him to New York, where he met my mother. If World War II hadn't happened, he would not have met her. We can see where this leads. To affirm my current situation seems to require that I affirm everything that led up to it, which seems to be the entirety of human history as it has unfolded in the particular way that it has.

If our ground projects are sources of affirming our lives, if they are what give our lives the meaning they have, then we must, in order to preserve that meaning, affirm the entirety of human history—or something close to it. For instance, I, and many or most of us currently living, would not have existed without the occurrence of the Holocaust. Therefore, in order to affirm our lives we cannot completely regret the Holocaust. In the end we must affirm it.

If such an attitude were necessary, it would certainly constitute some form of nihilism. As Wallace notes, this form of nihilism need not be a rejection of any form of belief or affirmation. In fact, it requires a certain affirmation in order to get off the ground: affirmation of one's life, or at least one's ground project. Rather, he argues, the problem is one of what he calls "anxiety." "It is anxiety about meaning, rather than resignation or other more theatrical forms of adjustment in orientation, that is the real hallmark of nihilism in the contemporary world. . . . Anxiety about meaning, on this interpretation, derives from our recognition that the deep aspiration to live lives that are worthy of unconditional affirmation may not be realizable at the end of the day."[8] This does not imply, as a more radical nihilism would, that there is no point to our living or that we cannot make a difference in the world. We can engage in activities that, to one extent or another, offset some of the more egregious conditions that led us to where we are. We can make the world better. But we cannot ultimately live in ways that deny that we are the product of horrific historical circumstances, circumstances which we must affirm in the sense of not having all-in regret about them. Without the Holocaust, I wouldn't even be here.[9]

We should note that this nihilism is compatible with affirming the better aspects of human history. If my existence is dependent on the whole of human history—or at least much of it—it may also be dependent on the existence of Shakespeare, Gandhi, the women's suffrage movement, the Renaissance, and basketball. And I get to affirm all these as well—in fact, I must. But then I find myself in the uncomfortable position of affirming these things and also the Holocaust, and then wondering whether they were all worth the suffering the latter involved. As Ivan says to Alyosha in Dostoyevsky's *The Brothers Karamazov*, "if the sufferings of children go to swell the sum of sufferings which is necessary to pay for truth, then I protest that the truth is not worth such a price."[10]

I would like to avoid having to embrace Wallace's view. That view, it seems to me, is the flip side of the invulnerabilism of the previous chapter. If invulnerabilism asks us to be unaffected by the past, at least in our emotions, Wallace demands that we be abject before it. Given our attachment to our own lives, we must simply say yes to everything that has happened that brought us about, Holocaust and all. Neither the invulnerabilists nor Wallace would allow for us to grapple with the past, take up a more nuanced, if more emotionally vexed, attitude toward it. What I would like to do here is suggest that just as we needn't be invulnerabilists, neither need we be nihilists, modest or otherwise. There is a third path open to us. This path will eventually allow us to conceive our lives as both fraught and yet not entirely bereft, as lives that are fragile but not necessarily broken.

In asking whether we are forced into Wallace's "modest nihilism," we should first recall that the structure of the bourgeois predicament, particularly as it concerns the past, is different from that of the young mother or the imagined Gauguin. In the latter two cases, the affirmation dynamic arises in regard to an action performed by the person herself or himself. The girl affirms her going through with her pregnancy, while Gauguin affirms his leaving his family. (The girl might have regretted getting pregnant in the first place, at least at the time, but going through with the pregnancy was an active choice.) By contrast, the bourgeois professor did not choose the past acts on which her current situation is based. I did not participate in the Holocaust or for that matter in anything my parents did before I was born. Therefore, if I am affirming something, whatever it is, it cannot be a refusal of all-in regret for something *I did*.

If I did not cause the Holocaust to happen, then in what sense am I required to affirm it—that is, to have a preference for the Holocaust to have happened? There is clearly one sense in which I am *not* required to affirm it. We might call it a moral sense. I can say, while still being attached to my own life, that would be better for the Holocaust not to have happened and for me not to have been born. That is to say, I am willing to affirm—and indeed I do affirm, as I suspect most of us will—that it would have been morally or impersonally better had the Holocaust not happened even at the cost of my existence. (To be clear here, this affirmation presupposes that, the Holocaust not having happened, nothing else happened that was worse. The reason to choose the Holocaust is precisely because it would have been difficult for history to produce much worse events—although, admittedly, history has proven to be creative in this regard.) That millions of people should have died in horrible ways in order that I might live is difficult to affirm as a morally good thing.

However, there is another sense of affirmation, different from a moral one, that might be associated with the idea of a preference for the Holocaust having happened. This other sense would be more closely associated with the term *preference*. Inasmuch as I prefer to be alive, with the life I am leading, am I not committed to affirming the conditions that led here, Holocaust included? Or, to put the point another way, does my preference for being here require that I also prefer the Holocaust to have happened, that I not regret that it happened, since it is necessary for it to have happened in order for me to be here?

Before addressing this question, we should note how far we are from any standard notion of regret. The regret that is being denied here in affirming the Holocaust would not be a refusal of the idea that the Holocaust is regrettable, in the sense we might say, in a much more superficial instance, that it is regrettable that a child had to be punished in order to learn her lesson—that is, that she needed to learn her lesson, there was no other way to do so than through punishment, and it is unfortunate that this had to be the case. One can hold both that it is regrettable that the Holocaust happened and that one prefers it to have happened because it led to my existence.

It seems to me, however, that we need not even have this kind of preference. It is not required of us. I might well say that my own existence was not worth it, that I would have preferred not to have been born if the Holocaust could have been avoided this way. To see why, let's first bear in mind what such a position would and would *not* entail. It does not entail sacrificing my life in any usual sense. I would not have had to die for the Holocaust not to have happened. Instead, I would not have come into existence. To be sure, the joys of this life—which I now know because I exist—would not have happened to me. But I wouldn't have missed those joys, for the simple reason that I wouldn't have been there to miss them.

On the surface, this may sound a lot like Epicurus's position that there is no reason to fear death because where death is, one is not, or perhaps Lucretius's extension of that argument to the idea that people do not regret the time before they were born. There are similarities. But there is also an important difference, one that makes it easier to prefer sacrificing my coming into being if that could have prevented the Holocaust. I share with Epicurus and Lucretius the idea that where one does not exist one cannot feel badly about not having the pleasures of existence. However, in Epicurus's view, we are asked to say the life to which we are already attached must not be a source of concern in the face of death, because we will no longer be there to be concerned. In the position I am taking, by contrast, we are asked not to be concerned about attachments *that would never have arisen*. It seems to me that the latter request is less onerous than the former one. In the case of never having been born, I am not asked to abandon the projects and pleasures of my life, since none of them would have happened in the first place. This seems to me to be an easier commitment to make than the one that requires leaving engagements that one has already formed.

Moreover, this request is bolstered by the recognition — one that has no analogy in Epicurus's case — that my inexistence is the result of the Holocaust's not happening. It is easier for me to say that I would have preferred not to have existed at the price of the Holocaust than to say that I should not worry about what I have become attached to because I won't be there after my death to be attached to those things. To be clear, I do not mean this distinction to be an argument against Epicurus but instead an argument that the position I am proposing is easier to occupy than Epicurus's.

I am also not arguing that such a view is required. Someone might, in fact, prefer the Holocaust to have happened in order that he would exist. Rather, my view is that such a preference is not necessary. But in order to make this case, I need to show not only that a person can prefer her own inexistence to the Holocaust but also that this does not require that she is not attached to her existence. That is, I need to show that although I can prefer not to have existed in the first place, if this would prevent the Holocaust from having happened, this does not mean that my existence is not important to me.

In fact, I am deeply attached to my own life: to my role as a philosopher, to my friends and family, and to several places where I feel a strong connection. I would not wish that this life, and indeed this particular life, had not happened to me. However, if I were told that I had the power somehow to go back in time and prevent the Holocaust at the cost of my own existence, I believe I would be capable of taking that bargain. I certainly hope so.

It might seem improbable that anyone would be able to

make such a sacrifice if her own life were at stake. However, we should remember first that many people *do* sacrifice their lives for things they consider important, lives that they already possess. And as we have seen, I would not be sacrificing a life that exists but instead simply not have come into existence. That seems to me to be a less difficult choice than sacrificing one's life.

Second, we should bear in mind what is on the other side of the ledger from my life. David Hume famously argued, and more recently the contemporary philosopher Shelly Kagan has deepened the argument, that vividness can sometimes act as moral motivation. As Kagan notes, "If I find myself in the presence of someone whose life is in danger, I will often be prepared to make some sort of sacrifice so as to provide aid. Yet I am rarely moved to make a comparable sacrifice when I am not faced with the individual himself, but merely have knowledge that there *is* a person in similar need of my aid."[11] Let's apply that thought to the Holocaust. When I visited the Holocaust Memorial Museum in Washington, I was able to get through many of the exhibits without breaking down and weeping. That is, until I got to the shoes. (I understand that I am not alone in this.) Seeing the shoes, many of them with worn leather and loose stitching, brought home to me the humanity and the vulnerability of those who suffered terrible fates at the hands of the Nazis. It was there, of all places in the museum, that their lives and their deaths became vivid to me. Of course, this was not the first time I was felled by a confrontation with the Holocaust, but in memory it remains one of the most significant. At that moment of vividness, I imagine it would not have been difficult to trade my existence for their lives.

One might object here that, given my attachment to my

own life, such a trade would have been irrational, especially at the moment I was standing in front of the shoes. It would have been a decision made in a moment of passion rather than after sober reflection. However, the passion in play at that moment was not an irrational one. It was not the passion resulting from, say, walking in on one's spouse in flagrante delicto, where one might do something one later regrets. Rather than an obscuring of the larger moral situation in the heat of the moment, that passion was an intimate contact with it. It was a realistic recognition of what the Holocaust was really about rather than an irrational feeling arising in me.

There is no reason, then, to say that I must affirm my life at the price of the Holocaust, or of any aspect of the past to which I owe my existence. The "modest nihilism" that Wallace thinks is inescapable for so many of us is not necessary. It is not our existential condition. We need not affirm the horrors that have preceded us. But if this is so, what would be the proper attitude toward the monstrosities on which our lives are built? How should we relate to them?

The attitude we might take up could perhaps be called one of *acceptance* rather than affirmation. In acceptance, I recognize that my existence and my current fortunate position in life are grounded in a history that has many horrors. I would not be here and would not be able to enjoy my position without those horrors having happened. The fact that, because they preceded me, I could do nothing about them ought not to make me feel indifferent toward them or fail to recognize their necessity in my coming into being. However, that I can do nothing to ameliorate those horrors does not require me either to affirm them or to withdraw an attachment to my own life. I do not affirm what I cannot have changed. I accept that it happened. I recognize the role it has played in producing a decent life for me. In moments of vividness I am aware that I should, and perhaps would, have given my good fortune to prevent some of these horrors. But I cannot prevent them, so while I do not affirm a life based on them I accept it.

This acceptance, unlike the affirmation dynamic, is not the refusal of all-in regret. If it were, then I would not have been prepared to sacrifice my life for the salvation of the history that preceded me. Moreover, it does not have the character of regret that we looked at above. It can't, because I did not commit those acts. It is instead the recognition of an ultimately tragic character that attends to our existence. Our lives occur on the basis of atrocities we did not commit and cannot undo. We will never make better the lives of those who suffered before us and to whose suffering we owe our existence. We cannot even address them, much less redress what happened to them. And so we move on, carrying that recognition with us as one of the tragedies that underlies even what is best in the human endeavor.

But why, one might ask, wonder about the past in this way at all? Why ask myself what I might do about circumstances I could not have had any control over? The Holocaust happened. There is nothing I can do to make it un-happen. Instead of focusing hypothetically on what I might have done, given the opportunity, why not turn my attention instead to what I might do in the future?

There are two responses to this, one more general and one specific to the discussion here. The general answer is that we often ask ourselves what we might have done in situations that are already past so that we can learn about how to act in the future. "If I were in her shoes I would have . . ." is not an uncommon reflection. We know that we cannot be in her shoes, and certainly could not have been in them at a past time. And yet, we allow our reflections on these hypothetical matters to guide us in our thinking—and, one hopes, our action—in future circumstances.

More specifically, we are asking about what attitude we might take to our own lives. By reflecting on the Holocaust, we prize apart an attitude—acceptance—from something with which it might be confused—affirmation. This will allow us to see our way to an alternative to invulnerabilism that is not some form of "modest nihilism." The twists and turns of our considerations here have allowed us to put that attitude before us. To be sure, our reflections have been a little more hypothetical and certainly more emotionally vexed than "If I were in her shoes I would have. . . ." But they have secured us a concept that allows us to move forward. If Wallace is right that I would not give my existence to have prevented the Holocaust (or some other monstrosity of our history), then we must be "modest nihilists." By testing ourselves against this hypothetical example, and by recognizing that we need not affirm our existence against the Holocaust, we have seen our way to a relation to the past that will, in the next chapter, allow us to develop a more general attitude toward the vulnerability of our lives.

My good fortune, then, and the good fortune of many of us, is built on a history that is too often monstrous. We can, and we ought, to seek to make the future less monstrous. We do so, however, not to make up for our existence, as though we made some mistake. Rather, we learn from the history that produced us so that we do not contribute to what we wish would not have happened. This is very different from the affirmation dynamic as Wallace understands it. In his concluding chapter, he recommends several courses of action in the face of the bourgeois predicament. "One of these is that there should be something in our lives that can be set over and against the objectionable conditions we inhabit, something that gives us a positive basis for affirming our lives when we look back on them. . . . A second important ambition for our lives concerns their moral quality. . . . It matters to us that we should interact with people on terms that are acceptable to them. . . . Finally, there is a still more specific value that we can reasonably aspire to achieve in our lives . . . which is the value of truthfulness."[12]

None of these ambitions, it seems to me, is an unreasonable one for a life to take. But neither should they be "set over and against the objectionable conditions we inhabit." If those conditions are current ones, then we should, as we saw earlier, struggle against them. And such struggle, as I argued, does not necessarily further implicate us in a bourgeois predicament. By contrast, if those conditions are past ones, then it would not make sense to make up for our existence through these projects. First, we cannot ameliorate the suffering of those who came before us, so we cannot make up to them for, or through, our existence. Second, although we owe our existence and good fortune in part to their suffering, there is nothing really to make up for. In accepting rather than affirming our lives, we have not ratified their suffering, so there is nothing that needs to be "set over and against" it.

Let me conclude with a final challenge to my view, one that may have already struck the reader in the discussion of the willingness to "sacrifice" life to prevent the Holocaust. It might be pointed out that in forgoing my life, I would not only be eliminating it but also the lives of those that my life produced. In short, had I not existed, neither would my children. It could then be asked of me whether I would be willing to forgo their existence in order to have prevented the Holocaust. And this, I must admit, is a more wrenching question.

In approaching it, the first thing to note is that I must recognize, as I did at the outset of the reflection on my own life, that from an impartial moral perspective the answer is that it is better that my children would not have come into existence if that would have prevented the Holocaust. I do not think of this as an uncomfortable recognition. One can endorse morally what one does not prefer, and so it seems that I—and for that matter my children (who are no longer children)—could ratify the view that their existence does not justify the occurrence of the Holocaust.

The question with more bite has to do not with moral recognition but with preference. Would I prefer that my children had not come into existence, if that would have somehow retroactively prevented the Holocaust? And as we consider this question, we should bear in mind that to affirm their existence would also require affirming mine, and thus would indirectly undercut the argument I made earlier about forgoing my own existence. Inasmuch as my existence would be necessary for my children's existence, to affirm my children's existence at the price of the Holocaust would require affirming my own as a condition of their existence.

My response is that it is not for me to say what I prefer here. It is for each of my children to say. If, for instance, my children said they would not prefer their existence at the price of the Holocaust, I would respect that; and if they said the opposite, I would respect that as well. This respect is not an affirmation but rather a deferring to them—and so it might seem to dodge the issue. However, to respect the decisions of those one loves in matters of their own deepest personal concerns is not, it seems to me, to contrive a convenient way out of a dilemma or a difficult decision but instead to place that decision where it belongs. Do I have a deep preference that my children exist? Of course. Do I have a deep preference for the Holocaust not to have happened? Of course. Do these conflict? Of course. To choose between them is not for me, however, but for those whose (admittedly hypothetical) stakes are at issue.

Someone might further object here, though, that there is a possibility that, given my children's preferences, I might still be forced to affirm my own existence in the wake of the Holocaust. Suppose that one or more of my offspring said that it was worth the Holocaust for them to come into existence. In respecting their choice, would I not be forced to affirm my own existence as a necessary condition of theirs? I do not see that this is required. One can respect a decision without either agreeing or disagreeing with it. And in matters this vexed, it seems that this is the right course of action. To say that I respect my children's decisions that their existence is worth the Holocaust is not to say that I now affirm the Holocaust as a necessary condition of my own and therefore their existence. It is only to say that I understand how one can come to such a view, and that it is not necessary for them to change it. It might be different from mine, but it is not necessarily wrong for all that. The two are not in conflict.

A last objection, I suppose, might be this. Since it is necessary that my children exist in order to have a view on the matter one way or another, do I not have to affirm my existence as a condition of their even having a view of the matter? Here again, I don't think affirmation is necessary. The fact is, my children exist. Since they exist, it is up to them to deal with this difficult matter in their own way, assuming they choose to deal with it at all. If they didn't exist, there would be no problem facing them of how to think about their relation to the horrors that produced them. The issue arises only because they exist in the first place. So the proper starting point is not the affirmation of my existence in order that, in turn, they can exist and so can ask themselves a question whose answer I will respect. The proper starting point is their existence itself, which requires neither affirmation nor regret. It is simply a condition of their being able to ask themselves the question of their relation to the past that gave rise to them.

Acceptance, in the way that we have developed the term here, requires a more nuanced attitude toward the past than either Wallace's modest nihilism or the rejection of any concern with the past associated with invulnerabilism. For Wallace, we are required to affirm the past, which lands us in his modest nihilism. By contrast, for invulnerabilism, concern with the past is unwarranted. There is only the present. The past does not exist and so is of no concern to us, except perhaps to offer us lessons on how to exist more fully in the present. As I have mentioned, these attitudes are related, sharing the assumption that one must either embrace or relinquish the past. Acceptance is neither nihilist nor invulnerabilist. It is, instead, an attitude that is vulnerable to the past, recognizing and taking seriously the horrors on which our own lives are based. However, it does not require that we affirm those horrors. In that way, it steers a course between nihilism and invulnerabilism, seeing our existence as fraught—neither requiring affirmation of the past nor admitting escape from it. We are compromised but not necessarily fallen.

With the concept of acceptance in hand, the question we must turn to is how a life that is neither invulnerabilist nor nihilist might look in its larger character, not simply in its relation to the past. What is it to live vulnerably but not nihilistically, and in particular to be able to take on the lessons of invulnerabilism—of which there are many—without taking on the invulnerability it commends? How do we live in such a way as to recognize our own fragility without seeking to escape it while at the same time not making ourselves abject before it? It is to this final task that we now turn.

LIVING VULNERABLY

How might we live with our vulnerability? How might we take on grief and failure, physical limitations and psychological scars, the weight of the past and the future? How might we take these on without either making ourselves immune to them or succumbing to the burdens they place on us? In short, how might we learn to live with our suffering?

Thought about in one way, these are odd questions. They would presuppose that living vulnerably is a task, a project, and in that way (although not in others) like living invulnerably. But it's not. Living vulnerably is not the mirror image of living invulnerably. It is not a particular kind of task or project.

Recall from the first chapter the idea of a project and its relation to practices. A project is a practice or a group of practices that a person identifies with over time. To live invulnerably is a project. In fact, for many who choose to live that way, it is a ground project in the sense that the philosopher Bernard Williams uses the term. Why is this? People do not naturally live invulnerably. We suffer from our physical and psychological debilities, from our regrets about what might have been and the cold face of our inevitable end. And we suffer from the injuries and wrongs undergone by those we care about. If we are to live invulnerably we must figure out how to get beyond the suffering that is natural to us.

How do we do this? Through a set of practices that will render us invulnerable to our suffering. Of course we need not render ourselves invulnerable to things like the pain of stubbed toes. But if we are to overcome real suffering, then we need to engage in practices that will help us achieve this. The practices commended by the invulnerabilists are dedicated precisely to the overcoming of suffering. Some of these practices are specific to one or more of the views we have canvassed. Meditation is a Buddhist practice, but not a Stoic or Epicurean one. Alternatively, imagining the death of a loved one, recommended by Epictetus, is not among the practices of Buddhism, although the story of Masters Li and Lai in Chuang Tzu come very close to it.

On the other hand, there are commonalities among the invulnerabilist practices, probably none more so than focusing on the present moment. Each view, in its own way, seeks to recognize what Tolle calls the power of now. By inhabiting the present fully one can get past regrets for what has happened and fear or anxiety for what is to come. Buddhist conceptions of desire, Stoic conceptions of passion, Taoist concerns with the binaries of language, Epicurean unnecessary desires: all of these can fall away if we turn from what has occurred or might occur to what is occurring now. But inhabiting the present moment, as all of these views recognize, requires a commitment over time to overcoming how we might otherwise feel and act.

These are the practices that must be engaged in to become an invulnerabilist of one type or another. They are to be taken up not only as practices, but as projects, and more important as core or central projects. This is not only because suffering is natural to us. It is also because suffering can happen within all (or almost all) of our other projects. We have come to recognize this over the course of the previous chapters. Suffering lies in wait for us in many of the things we care about, whether it is our accomplishments or our desires or our friends and loved ones. It needn't arise in any of these and, if we are lucky, will not arise at all. But it can. And because it can, invulnerabilism must spread its immunity across our other projects. This requires it to become a central project, a project that we take up as a fundamental one in our lives. To live invulnerably is to live with a release from suffering in our careers, our families, our friendships, our hobbies, our religions, and so on. So it cannot happen unless we are committed to the project of invulnerability both in the specific practices it offers and in allowing it to spread its effects across our other projects.

This is why many people who strike us as invulnerable often seem to have precisely that invulnerability as their central characteristic. Their serenity in the face of the world's vicissitudes, the distance they secrete between themselves and its occasional onslaughts: this is often what strikes the observer of those who have mastered or are seeking to master their suffering. Someone might ask whether it is not simply the rarity of such a characteristic that attracts our attention. Indeed, such figures are rare. But that rare characteristic would not stand out were it not for the fact that it pervades their other projects. They are unflappable at their jobs, in their relationships, and in their daily movement through the world. So while real invulnerability is rare, its appearance in an individual pervades the way they navigate through life.

Invulnerability as a central project in this way stands in contrast to vulnerability. The latter is not a project. We do not seek to become vulnerable. Rather we are vulnerable. We suffer in the face of loss, failure, moral conflict, and physical debility. We are weighed down by anxiety or depression or stress or regret. Vulnerability is our natural state. This does not mean, of course, that we are always suffering, or that we must suffer to the extent that we do. It means rather that unless we actively do something to struggle against it—unless we make it a project—we are exposed to the possibility of suffering in many arenas of our life. Vulnerability, then, is not a project that one might choose instead of choosing invulnerability for the simple reason that it is not a project at all.

This contrast leads to another one. There is a diversity to living vulnerably that makes it more difficult to categorize than any variety of invulnerabilism, or even invulnerabilism as a whole. We can see why this is if we linger a moment over the centrality of invulnerabilism to those who embrace it. Whether Buddhist or Taoist or Stoic or (to some extent) Epicurean or a follower of Tolle's regimen, someone who subscribes to invulnerabilism makes it a central project, a core aspect of who she is. This is because, as we have seen, people are vulnerable in so many aspects of life that invulnerabilism must make its way into all those aspects. Invulnerabilist lives, then, exhibit a central common trait: serenity in the face of all potential suffering. However, suffering comes in many forms, as we have seen. Therefore, a life that allows itself to be vulnerable to suffering is often going to display more diversity in regard to suffering than one that exhibits serenity in the face of such suffering. Here one is reminded of Tolstoy's opening words to his great novel *Anna Karenina*: "All happy families resemble one another; each unhappy family is unhappy in its own way."

As a result, it is more difficult to characterize vulnerabilism than invulnerabilism. There is no doctrine of vulnerabilism in the sense that there are doctrines of invulnerabilism. If vulnerabilism has a central claim, it would be something as general and as unhelpful as "Don't make yourself invulnerable to suffering, but, at least most of the time, don't make yourself abject to it either." Or, as we will see, "Accept as best you can your vulnerability." Anything more specific would risk understating the various ways in which suffering can occur. In this sense, vulnerabilism shares with Buddhism at least the first Noble Truth: life is (or at least can be) sorrowful. (Vulnerabilism can also be said to share the second Noble Truth, that sorrow comes from craving, as long as craving is taken in the very wide sense of human desire, which is the way much of Buddhism seems to take it.)

That vulnerabilism does not have a very specific central claim or set of claims is related to its not having a central project. There is no particular way vulnerabilism asks us to be, and therefore no particular action it asks us to take. What characterizes vulnerabilism is not so much its embrace of a particular form of life as its rejection of one. What vulnerabilism commends is living in a way that allows one to be vulnerable to suffering. And since that allowance concerns something that is natural in any event, it doesn't require a project to achieve it. It is the rejection of a project—that of invulnerabilism—that characterizes the vulnerabilist approach to life rather than the commitment to an alternative project.

If this is true, however, does it leave us without the ability to say anything about vulnerabilism? Are we left with nothing more than the negative statement that vulnerabilism is the rejection of invulnerabilism? That would not be very helpful in thinking about our lives. To be sure, it would be something. After all, knowing that we have the option of not seeking to make ourselves immune to suffering, given the problems with such a project, opens up a distinct way for us to view our lives. However, to say of that distinct way, "Well, it involves allowing oneself to suffer," is pretty thin pickings. Given the diversity of vulnerable lives and the fact that vulnerabilism is not a project in anything like the way invulnerabilism is, must we stop our reflections there?

As it turns out, we needn't. It is one thing to say that vulnerabilism is not a project and that there are many ways to live vulnerably. It is quite another to claim that we must remain silent about what those ways are like. We have opened at least two paths of reflection in trying to characterize what we are calling vulnerable lives, lives that are neither immune to nor entirely given over to suffering. First, we can say some general things about vulnerable lives, things that would apply across the diversity of such lives. There are vulnerabilist *themes*, if not a particular vulnerabilist project. We can sketch outlines of some of those themes. Second, we can give examples of vulnerabilism as distinct from invulnerabilism. In fact, we have already done so in our critique of invulnerabilism. Issues around politics, death, failure, and grief are examples of where a vulnerable life would differ from an invulnerable one. As this chapter progresses we will have more to say about some of these examples.

As we embark on these reflections, let us bear in mind two things. First, we need not take the position that no one should live invulnerably or take on invulnerabilism as a project. The difficulties we have cited for invulnerabilism provide reasons why many of us—probably most—would not want to follow the invulnerabilist path. There is, however, nothing morally wrong or depraved with invulnerabilism. It hardly makes someone who seeks to be invulnerable to suffering worse than someone who does not. Those who find invulnerabilism attractive need not be discouraged from pursuing the life it offers. In fact, if vulnerabilism is characterized by a diversity of ways of living, the addition of invulnerabilism as a way of living will only add to that diversity.

Second, the rejection of invulnerabilism is not the rejection of all its aspects. There are aspects of invulnerabilism that can be brought into vulnerabilism. Or, to put the point another way, the rejection of immunity to suffering does not require the rejection of immunity to some suffering, or even much suffering. There are many things we suffer over that, in retrospect (and even some times in prospect), we recognize are not worth the suffering we undergo. Taking on some of the lessons of invulnerabilism will help us deal with those. In fact, in characterizing vulnerabilist lives, we can start with a distinction that will immediately allow us to take on board themes from invulnerabilism.

We have insisted that vulnerabilism, while not pursuing an exemption from suffering, does not ask us to embrace suffering in all its forms. There are things we suffer over that we would prefer not to, or things other people suffer over that we want to say are not really worth it. For my own part, I am a bit of a control freak. Although on the one hand I hanker after new situations and challenges, on the other hand I often feel the need to be in control of what's going on around me. It's not only that, like a lot of parents, I have difficulty refraining from offering helpful advice to my grown offspring in areas they don't need it. I hate being late, so I will often take early trains and busses in order to avoid the tardiness that would come with an unexpected delay, only to find myself wandering around aimlessly to kill time before a meeting. In meetings or in organizations I am tempted to take hold of things in order to ensure that they move along correctly and efficiently. I schedule my days to make sure that I know what I'm doing each hour. Of course, none of these things is bad in itself. However, whenever I'm going to be late or am in a disorganized meeting or can't accomplish something I've scheduled myself to do, I become anxious or irritable. This is so even when I can't control the reasons any of these things are happening. That, of course, is what a control freak is: when I can't control a situation, I freak. (Okay, I rarely actually freak, but I rarely fail to become anxious either.)

There is no need for this. Sometimes I even tell myself as much. I am sure I am not the first person to stand in a stalled train on the way to a meeting with people whose phone numbers I don't possess, telling myself there's nothing I can really do about this, but to no noticeable emotional effect. What I need to recognize, not simply "in my head" but in my entire body, is that this delay is not a big deal. It will at worst cause annoyance in others, an annoyance that will likely fade when the cause for the delay becomes known. And if the annoyance remains, that's okay as well. It is also okay to have meetings that are less organized than I would like or to miss the reading I have assigned myself on this particular Tuesday or to forget to give my grown children a bit of advice that they either won't need or won't listen to anyway or to stay relaxed when I hear the car engine make the kind of noise that car engines are not supposed to make while I'm on the way to work.

These are what might be called Small Matters. They are not worth getting upset about. The reason for this is not simply that I can't control them. As we will see, there are things I can't control that may well be worth my being upset or even devastated about, things worth regretting or grieving. The little things I often fret over are not among them. And part of wisdom, particularly vulnerabilist wisdom, lies in knowing the difference between Small Matters and Large Matters.

Before going any further, however, we should linger over a complication that might be imported from our earlier discussion of the weight of the past. It is not clear that what appear to be Small Matters are all that small. For instance, if I'm standing on a train getting annoyed I might spend a few minutes at work or home telling someone about it. That could change the arrangement of sperm in my body such that when my wife conceives it is with a different sperm from the one she would have otherwise conceived with. As a result, we have a different child from the one we would have had if I had been more relaxed on the train. We need not imagine radically different future life trajectories for these children in order to recognize that the difference between being annoyed and not being so could lead to the production of different lives. And if this is right, how can we be sure in any given case of the difference between the Small and the Large? And if we can't do that, how can we develop wisdom in regard to that difference?

You will immediately recognize this as what has come to be called the Butterfly Effect. A butterfly flaps its wings, and the air currents from this have an effect that, through a series of intermediary effects, changes the course of history. Its bearing on our current reflection is that it seems to undermine the distinction between Small Matters and Large Matters, leaving us without the ability to develop any sense of proportion about our lives. However, there is a sense of proportion we can develop *about the Butterfly Effect*, one that also stems from our discussion of the weight of the past. There we saw that one simply cannot know what an alternative life would have looked like. Our choices are made in a necessary ignorance of paths other choices would have led us on. This does not mean that we cannot affirm our life, but, as we saw, that affirmation—like its opposite, regret—has an unusual character, since it cannot be done comparatively.

In the case of the weight of the past, the affirmation or regret is retrospective, even though its effects could extend into one's future. In the situations we're considering here—those of Small Matters—the choices are made contemporaneously. We are not looking back on times when we have been in ignorance of where we might have been and where those previous choices might lead us in the future. Instead, we are asking ourselves how to act at the present moment, although also in ignorance of where those choices might eventually lead us. We might choose to become anxious about all this: that will be the path of the control freak. Alternatively, we can adopt another attitude. We might say that, since we cannot tell the future, what distinguishes a Small Matter from a Large Matter is not that we *know* the former to be Small and the latter to be Large but rather that their immediate effects appear to be Small and Large, respectively, and we have no idea what will happen beyond that.

There is a term we can invoke from the previous chapter to describe this attitude: *acceptance*. Although we invoke it with a slightly different nuance here, it has an important connection with what we have seen and what is to come. In the previous chapter, we saw that acceptance recognizes that many of us benefit from aspects of our history that we would not affirm but that we cannot change. We may wish this history were otherwise, even at the cost of our not being here, but we cannot go back in time and change it. The acceptance we are discussing here also recognizes that there are things we cannot control. In this case it is that in the longer term there may be consequences of what seem like unimportant matters that we cannot predict and therefore cannot control for. We accept this because what else can we do? We accept the uncertainty of our future as we accept the tragic character of our past because both are out of our control.

Acceptance here is beyond either regret or affirmation. We can neither regret nor affirm what has not yet happened and what, in any event, we do not and cannot know. We are helpless before an unforeseeable future. Whether our actions will have future consequences that are important either in a positive or a tragic way is knowledge to which we do not have access. We can do nothing other than recognize this ignorance for what it is and act on what we can control and according to the way things present themselves to us. And some things present themselves to us, or do when we reflect on them, as Small Matters. How then might we approach matters that seem more trivial or insignificant?

I am standing on a train that is late. Let's say it is a subway where I have no access to cell service. I will be late for a meeting with some colleagues who will be waiting for me, but there is at this point nothing I can do about it. How might I deal with my situation? There are several ways. I might ask, with Eckhart Tolle, is there anything wrong at this particular moment? (In fact, I have done this periodically, with spotty success. Recall that I am a control freak.) Or I might slow my breathing and meditate. I might tell myself that there is no reason to allow myself to be thrown off emotionally, because I cannot control the situation. Or I might inculcate in myself the recognition that in the larger scheme of things my being late to a meeting does not really matter. All of these exercises, it seems to me, are appropriate to the situation. They would put things in perspective. Lateness to a meeting is rarely cause for great concern. There might be annoyance with me, but unless the meeting itself is of great moment—which most of our meetings are not—my lateness is, at least in itself and abstracting from further consequences I cannot control, a Small Matter.

There are many aspects of my life that are like this. I believe I am not alone here. We live in an age of technology, and technology periodically fails us. Cell phones break, cars won't start, washing machines leak, elevators get stuck, power goes out during storms, wireless service gets interrupted, printers jam, flights get canceled because of technical glitches. None of this is surprising and rarely does any of it rise to the level where we should be terribly upset about it. But we often are, far more so than we should be, as we may realize in retrospect.

And technology is just the beginning of it. Strangers step on our toes unintentionally or bump us on the street. Waiters or store clerks can be abrupt with us because they are having their own personal difficulties. Doctors keep us waiting, sometimes (although admittedly not always) because of more pressing medical issues with other patients. Our kids get on our nerves over concerns that we want to tell them aren't important. There are ice storms, traffic jams, colleagues who are perennially irritating, slow periods at work, and so on. Almost always, if we look back on these things, we recognize them as matters we need not have become vexed over, matters we could not control and need not have become upset about. They are Small Matters. How might we otherwise deal with them?

Here is where the wisdom of invulnerabilism begins to show itself. Without having to take on the idea that all suffering can or should be overcome, we can recognize that, in much of our daily lives, suffering is both self-imposed and unnecessary. We become anxious in regard to things we can do nothing about and, in our more lucid moments, realize will not matter much if they do occur (barring long-term effects that we cannot even begin to calculate). We also become unsettled about remote possibilities that, even if they would be terrible, are very unlikely to happen. When our grown kids travel to other countries or our spouse meets an attractive person for dinner or our workplace undergoes reorganization or our friend moves into a neighborhood that is transitional but still dangerous, something bad could happen. But it's not likely and it seems pointless to worry about it. It would be a mistake to say we needn't be concerned in the sense that there is nothing that could happen that would be of concern. It would probably be right, however, to say that we needn't worry ourselves with it.

How do we overcome our unnecessary or pointless suffering? Here are a number of ways. One way, common to many invulnerabilist views (as Tolle has noted), is to focus on the present. We can ask ourselves, "Is anything wrong at this moment?" Often, the answer is no. And in the kinds of situations we're talking about, the answer is always no. We can reflect on our concern, noticing it as concern and so distancing ourselves from it. We can also approach the present in a positive manner. We can focus on what is positive in the moment we are inhabiting: the book we are reading, the way the leaves play in the sunlight, the stillness of the early evening or, in a city, the white noise of motion around us. If someone is with us, we can be with him or her, not just physically but with our entire being. We can ask ourselves what we can control in the present, and go about controlling it. Or, alternatively, we can ask ourselves whether the thing we are anxious about can be controlled and, if not, then gently let it go. And if we want to make such an approach to the present more of a habit in our lives, we can learn to meditate. Or, more broadly, we can engage in what the philosopher of ancient thought Pierre Hadot calls "spiritual exercises."

Hadot offers a view of ancient philosophy as importantly different from contemporary academic philosophical work. We tend to think of philosophers, not incorrectly, as academic workers concerned with conceptual matters. Philosophers are usually employed at universities, teaching a general overview of the field to undergraduates and more specialized views to graduate students, publishing books that will be read by few people or articles that will be read by even fewer, adding their own detail or nuance to a field already overcrowded with these little cognitive baubles. It is not that there is no room for specialization in philosophy. Philosophical thinking can be difficult and sometimes it needs to be technical. But it is easy to lose sight of the philosophical point of one's work and to think of it solely from within the field of academic philosophical discussion. Worse, one's work can be considered as nothing more than a stepping stone to tenure or to a position at a better university or a way to have an impact on "the field."

I doubt that many of us who have careers as philosophers went into it thinking that the point of it all was to enjoy a certain position in the academic world. Instead, we were moved by questions that puzzled or concerned us: How should we live? What is just or unjust? Can we know anything at all? What is human nature? And yet, formed by the practice in which we're engaged, we often allow ourselves to be molded into creatures who treat philosophy the same way business people treat their careers: as paths leading to professional advancement.

Hadot argues that ancient Western philosophers saw themselves very differently. (Although he does not discuss this, the same holds true for Eastern philosophers.) For them, what was at stake was not an intellectual contribution to the field of philosophy. Rather, the issue for ancient philosophers was solely one of how to live. A philosopher was not simply a person who propounded a specific philosophical position. And being a philosopher didn't require that one introduce a novel view or a new position. A philosopher was someone who lived in accordance with a philosophical doctrine. Someone could be a philosopher without having written or thought anything original. Rather, one molded one's life self-reflectively in accordance with a larger philosophical view and thereby became a philosopher. To be sure, Plato and Aristotle and Epicurus and Marcus were philosophers. But so were those who followed them, those whose names are lost to history but who tried to fashion their living in conformity to a wider doctrine of living that they found to be compelling. As Hadot tells us, for Stoics (and, as he goes on to discuss, for other ancient Western schools) "philosophy did not consist in teaching an abstract theory—much less in the exegesis of texts—but rather in the art of living. It is a concrete attitude and determinate life-style, which engages the whole of existence."[1] In that sense, today's Buddhists and Stoics are more nearly philosophers in the ancient sense Hadot discusses than many who are employed in contemporary philosophy departments.

What are spiritual exercises? They are the daily routines we engage in whose goal is to make us into the kind of being our chosen philosophy endorses. They seek to turn us from seeker into sage. Accomplishing this requires not simply a one-time commitment to being say, an Epicurean or a Stoic. Rather, it requires exercise, repeated daily, in order to sediment in us the characteristics proper to one's chosen philosophy. As Hadot tells us, "just as, by dint of repeated physical exercises, athletes give new form and strength to their bodies, so the philosopher develops his strength of soul, modifies his inner climate, transforms his vision of the world, and, finally, his entire being."[2] In short, if we are to become Stoics or Epicureans (or Buddhists or Taoists), we must habituate ourselves into that way of being.

The reason for this is not far to seek. We are not naturally prone to emotional detachment, simple desires, recognizing that we have no self, or avoiding the snares of language. We are naturally caught up in the world, engaged with its language and its workings, desiring and hoping to attain certain outcomes rather than others, caring about what happens to us and to others. If we are to get beyond all this, then we need to train ourselves to be otherwise. This does not happen through a single flash of insight but instead, as the ancients recognized, through a slow habituation that reorients our cognitive and emotional lives.

(I should insert, parenthetically, a quick explanation of the term *natural* invoked in the previous paragraph and in earlier pages in this chapter. To say that we are naturally prone to value our attachments does not mean that it is a necessary part of human nature or that it is unaffected by culture or history. The ancients probably thought so, but we needn't. We can say that these attachments arise as a part of human nature, or that they emerge solely through social influences, or that they come from a combination of the two. The debate about nature vs. environment is not at stake here. So we should understand the term *natural* here to mean something like "what we normally do in the course of things" rather than "what lies in the deep core of human existence.")

Many of us are tempted by the thought that life changes happen through a single epiphany, a "road to Damascus" moment. We hear or say of a single event, "That changed my life," "The scales fell from my eyes," or "I was never the same after that." However, such epiphanies are the exception rather than the rule. In his essay "Reprieve," the writer and cartoonist Tim Kreider captures this idea well. After having a near-death experience—he was stabbed in the throat—Kreider spent months feeling that every day was a gift, enjoying the moment and feeling grateful to be alive. However, that feeling gradually faded, no matter his efforts to retain it. "But now that I'm back in the slog of everyday life, I have to struggle to keep things in what I still insist is their true perspective. I know intellectually that all the urgently pressing items on our mental lists—our careers, car repairs, the daily headlines, the goddamned taxes—are just so much noise, that what matters is spending time with the people you love. It's just hard to bear in mind when the hard drive crashes or the shower drain clogs first thing in the day."[3]

What the ancient Western philosopher would say to Kreider here is that it is not enough to experience, however viscerally, a "true perspective." One has to incorporate it into the center of one's being. (For the ancient Eastern philosopher, it might be more proper to say that one must incorporate it into the center of one's nonbeing, or instead to realize that one has no center and that, ultimately, there is no one.) The path to this incorporation is that of spiritual exercises. We commit ourselves to a regimen of spiritual calisthenics with the goal of molding ourselves into the persons we would like to be. As we have seen, Marcus's *Meditations* opens with an example of such calisthenics: "Begin each day by telling yourself: Today I shall be meeting with interference, ingratitude, insolence, disloyalty, ill-will, and selfishness—all of them due to the offender's ignorance of what is good or evil." By doing this,

Marcus seeks to gird himself against his own irritation with others, irritation that will inevitably arise when he engages with those who have not overcome — or even hope to overcome — their passionate attachment to things of this world. In fact, Hadot points out, "One conception was common to all the philosophical schools: people are unhappy because they are the slave of passions."[4]

The exercises Hadot describes include meditation, being in the present, and especially coming to terms with death. These we have already seen. In addition, there are reading wise texts, concentrating on aphorisms, mentally focusing on pleasurable experiences (for the Epicurean), learning to dialogue with oneself as Socrates did, and contemplation of the universe and even the study of it as a divine creation. All of these exercises are ways of tearing ourselves away from the everyday involvements that catch us up in the world of our passions. They break the normal rhythm of life in order to cleave the attachments that rhythm fosters with the world. This in turn allows us to focus on the kind of person we want to be. Concentrating on aphorisms, for example, turns attention away from the world and toward the lesson that aphorism imparts. On the one hand, when I am contemplating the aphorism, I am no longer rapt by my own desire to control things or have them work out in ways I prefer. On the other hand, I am allowing that aphorism to speak to me, to be something other than words on a page or advice that passes through me without ever gaining a grip. Spiritual exercises have this twofold effect. They don't just block my natural engagement with the world; they also substitute for that engagement a way of being consonant with the person I would like to be, whether Stoic, Epicurean, Socratic, Buddhist, or Taoist.

The key to these exercises, however, is that, like physical

exercise, they must be done on a regular basis, daily if not more often. The truths they convey, as Hadot points out, are not conceptually difficult or abstract. As Hadot says, "[It is not that] old truths . . . are difficult; on the contrary, they are often extremely simple. Often, they even appear to be banal. Yet for their meaning to be understood, these truths must be *lived*, and constantly re-experienced. Each generation must take up, from scratch, the task of learning to read and re-read these 'old truths.'"[5] They must be engraved into our mental and behavioral repertoire, which requires repetition, just as muscle memory requires repeated physical exercises.

For ancient Western philosophers, especially the Stoics but, as we have seen, to a great extent the Epicureans, the goal of spiritual exercises is sagacity. One becomes a sage, and sages, in the sense sought by these doctrines, are immune to suffering. Even if we do not seek sagacity, however, we can benefit from these exercises or others like them. As most of us would readily admit, particularly in retrospect, we are vexed by troubles that too often are of our own making and that, given a second chance, we would approach differently. By engaging in spiritual exercises of the kind Hadot describes, we offer ourselves the opportunity to approach these aspects of our lives in prospect rather than regretting them in retrospect. We prepare for ourselves an equanimity that we can display moving forward rather than reproach ourselves for not having displayed it in the past.

All of this, however, concerns what I have called Small Matters, issues that are either of no great consequence or at least no great consequence of which we are aware. Not all matters are Small Matters. There are Large Matters, and, if we are not invulnerabilists, not only might we find it difficult to retain our tranquility in the face of their arising, we might not even want to. The division between vulnerabilism and invulnerabilism lies precisely there. It is not that the vulnerabilist rejects the project of equanimity entirely. Rather, it is that in certain Large Matters, the vulnerabilist does not seek, and does not want, tranquility. What she wants, and perhaps not at that moment but only down the road, is something we might call acceptance.

*

Friendships can fade in many ways. A friend of long standing, someone entwined with your life, moves to a foreign country. While email and even Skype allow for contact, you will never spend those leisurely Saturday mornings lingering over coffee or walking at dusk recounting the day's events: how the boss was a jerk yet again or that cute new dress is no longer on sale. Or perhaps this: one misunderstanding leads to another, and then another, and then it is difficult to trace your way back to that feeling of trust and comfort the (now former) friend's presence offered you. Or perhaps, worse: a car accident leaves your friend mentally incapacitated or cancer ushers her to an early death.

You can do little or nothing about these things. They happen against your wishes and your best efforts. Other things happen in this way as well. You value your integrity and sacrifice the worldly benefits that so often come with compromising it: the promotions that come with feigned praise to superiors or the recognition that hypocrisy often brings. Then you discover that your partner or spouse is embezzling at her workplace or your child has cheated on her college entrance exams or is selling drugs at her high school. Do you betray your partner or your child for the sake of your integrity? What if you believe that your child, who has struggled with bullying throughout high school, will thrive if she gets into a better college than the one she would have if she had not cheated? How do you at once salvage your integrity and express your love?

Other situations are simpler but just as far out of your control. You look back on your life and come to believe that it was a mistake. You took a path of safety because you were told to do so by your parents and your teachers, because you wanted the approval of others, because it was easy, or for any of a thousand other reasons that now seem as empty as the life you have led. Why didn't you accompany that friend who was driving to California just to see what it was like to live on the coast or take a chance with that startup company you were asked to join or major in English in college rather than accounting? After all, you loved reading novels on weekends while your peers played sports or drank beer.

Things could be simpler still. You struggle with anxiety and depression. The Queen of Darkness holds you in a full embrace and will not let you go. Or, like almost all of us, you die before you have lived as long and as passionately as you would have liked. What you would not give to wake up one more morning, watch the sun dapple the leaves outside your window, and hear the voices of those you love.

We care about what I have called our projects. Among those projects, we care deeply for the core or central projects of our lives. We intensely desire the flourishing of those we love, the success of those activities we are committed to, the values we seek for our lives to express. For most of us, that is what it means to care. Our caring lies not only in what we do but in what we feel, in what we desire for the objects of our care.

Moreover, that caring gives meaning to our lives. If we did not care in this way—care in the way of desire and passion, even if a quiet passion—then we would no longer be in the grip of our living. We would not feel our lives to be our own, something to which we felt attached. We would instead wear them like overcoats, soldiering through our days with our lives draped loosely around us. It is desire, passion, attachment that allow us to feel our lives to be ours rather than just something we happen to inhabit.

In short, for most of us caring involves attachment and lends meaning to our lives. Because of this, we are vulnerable to suffering.

In order to unpack these ideas, which are central to vulnerabilism, we should proceed in two steps. First we must establish the link between caring and suffering, then the link between caring and meaning. The first one, if we understand it rightly, is agreed on by both vulnerabilists and invulnerabilists. Central to caring about something is that it matters how the thing one cares about goes. We care about our friends and family; it matters to us whether they are flourishing or not. Many of us care about issues of social justice. It matters to us whether people are in needless poverty, suffering discrimination, or oppressed by their social order. When these things are happening, we suffer. For some of us, our caring leads to involvement in projects of social justice, and it matters to us whether those projects succeed. In a more pedestrian way, we prefer the engagements in our work lives to succeed—at least those of us whose work is significant to us, not just an alienating job. Imagine how you would feel if all of the ventures you participated in during your work life failed. Unless you are a committed invulnerabilist, this would matter to you. If part of caring about something is its mattering whether things go better or worse, then caring opens up the possibility of suffering.

That caring can lead to suffering might seem like an idea the invulnerabilist would reject. After all, we have seen that invulnerabilism allows for and even encourages compassion. One seeks to abandon one's selfish attachments and desires, often in favor of improving the lives of others. That is the role of the bodhisattva in Mahayana Buddhism. Stoicism displays a similar concern with its focus on acting justly toward others. These certainly seem to be forms of caring. If they are, isn't it possible to have caring without suffering, caring that partici-pates in the world without being attached to it?

Seeing things that way involves a confusion. We might call it a confusion between compassion and passion. Invulnerabil-ism often counsels compassion but never passion. That is to say, people ought to act in the interests of others but not be at-tached to the success or failure of that action. One is, to invoke a Hindu saying, entitled to his actions but not to the fruits of his actions. For invulnerabilists, it cannot matter whether projects succeed or fail. It cannot matter whether the lives of those around them go well or badly or whether there is a just social order. Of course one can say that it matters to them in the sense that they seek to better the lives around them or the social order in which they live. But for the invulnerabil-ist there must be a distance between what someone does and what she feels, and that is what we are getting at when we talk about caring. When a person becomes attached to what she is doing, to its object or its outcome, she is no longer hewing to the invulnerabilist creed, no matter which variety of that creed she endorses. What we are calling here caring renders people vulnerable to things they cannot control and therefore to suffering. It cannot be countenanced by invulnerabilism.

It might seem strange that someone would be asked to act with compassion on the one hand without it being able to matter whether that compassion is effective on the other. A person might ask the psychological question of what it must be like to act in a world she is not caught up with emotionally. What must it be like to be involved in a movement for women's rights or a struggle against the suicide of a friend and be able, should that movement or that struggle fail, to walk away unaffected? (Recall the discussion of Claus von Stauffenberg from the third chapter.) Once again, I do not say this is impossible. But it does seem psychologically unusual. Moreover, as we will see in a bit, it isn't something most of us would want. If we were able to walk away from such failures without sadness or remorse, then we might ask ourselves whether we really cared about the plight of women or the deceased friend. And that, I think, would be the right question.

Caring, then, since it involves mattering to someone how the cared about project or object fares, renders him vulnerable to suffering. Our second question is this: how does caring lend meaning to a life? In order to address this question, we need to say something about what makes a life meaningful.

Recently, the philosopher Susan Wolf has offered a view of what makes life meaningful that might help us here. The slogan she uses for her view is this: "meaning arises when subjective attraction meets objective attractiveness."[6] The idea is this: For a life to be meaningful, first of all it must engage us. A life in which we feel alienated is not a meaningful one. Imagine a painter, for instance, who creates beautiful paintings but feels utterly disconnected from them. She isn't even engaged by her work while she is painting. Instead she sees her activity simply as a means to make money to keep food on the table. Or think of people who are very decent morally but who feel alienated in their own lives. They strive to help others but feel an emptiness inside themselves. In Wolf's eyes, for our lives to be meaningful we must feel involved in what we're doing. That is what she means by subjective attraction.

But, says Wolf, subjective attraction is not enough. A person who is subjectively attracted solely to doing crossword puzzles or caring for her goldfish would not be living a meaningful life. She would not be taken up by something worthwhile, at least not worthwhile enough to stake her life projects on. Whatever the source of subjective attraction, then, it must be something worthy of attraction; it must be to something with "objective attractiveness."

Of course, we might wonder how one is to decide which projects are worthy of supporting meaning and which are not. Wolf herself has a very catholic approach to these projects; she appeals to very marginal examples in displaying lives that she thinks we would hesitate to call meaningful.

Now someone might be tempted to take issue with Wolf's claim that objective worthiness alone does not confer meaningfulness on a life. After all, the idea of a meaningful life lends itself to many interpretations. The alienated painter, for instance, might be said to be living a meaningful life—it just doesn't feel meaningful to her. For her part, Wolf is not concerned to counter such a claim. She is not wedded to the term *meaning*. What she is seeking to get at is a way of looking at or assessing a life that does not reduce to the traditional distinction between happiness and morality. She invokes the concept of meaning to capture this.

We need not defend Wolf's view here as being the only acceptable approach to understanding what makes a life meaningful. In fact, we might grant that a life without subjective attraction, a life in which one is not, as she puts it, "gripped, excited, interested, engaged,"[7] is still meaningful. Without saying that subjective attraction is *necessary* for a life to be meaningful, though, we can hold the more modest idea that subjective attraction enhances the meaningfulness of a life. To be sure, such attraction is not by itself sufficient, as Wolf herself has noted. But it helps. It could be, then, that an objectively attractive life is meaningful, but its meaning is augmented by subjective engagement. The painter's life, for instance, would be more meaningful if she felt moved by the art she creates or more involved in the process of creating it. I suspect that most of us would want to accord a more important role to subjective attraction than this modest one, but for our purposes we need not. We need only to say that subjective attraction *can* add meaningfulness to a life, and for most of us it does.[8]

But what is subjective attraction, if not caring? It is the involvement of someone in the project that is engaging or gripping her. And if she is involved in it, must not it matter to her how things go with that project or with its object? In introducing her view, Wolf writes, "When I visit my brother in the hospital, or help my friend move, or stay up all night sewing my daughter a Halloween costume, I act neither for egoistic reasons [i.e., happiness] nor for moral ones."[9] It is difficult to imagine these as examples of meaningfulness and not also imagine that it matters to her how her brother fares or whether the friend's house works out for him or whether her daughter feels sufficiently scary or charming in the Halloween costume. And although the failure of the latter two examples might lead simply to disappointment rather than suffering (they are Small Matters), the decline of her brother would probably cause her to suffer. This is not simply because he is her brother—after all, not all siblings care for each other. It is rather because she is subjectively attracted to the well-being of her brother, as evidenced by her visiting him in the hospital (assuming, of course, that the visit wasn't motivated solely by guilt or a sense of duty).

We can see the outcome of this line of thought. If, for most of us, a meaningful life involves subjective attraction, and if subjective attraction is a matter of caring, and if caring is, as we might say, a matter of mattering, and if mattering opens one up to suffering, then we can conclude that, for most of us, aspects of our lives that make them meaningful also open them to suffering. Meaningfulness does not require suffering—maybe we're just extraordinarily lucky and so never have to witness the failure of things we care about. But it does require—once again, for most of us—that we are open to the possibility that we will suffer. And in fact, since nearly all of us will at the very least face the death of a loved one, suffering seems nearly inescapable.

None of this is meant to deny that a life of invulnerability lacks meaning. What such a life does lack, however, is an important element of meaning: subjective attraction. And here the invulnerabilist might balk. Why should we assume that subjective attraction is a matter of caring, she might ask? Can't someone be "gripped, excited, interested, engaged" by a project without being vulnerable to suffer at its failure? (Bear in mind here that we are discussing the failure of Large Matters, not Small Matters.) In fact, as we have seen, Buddhists and Stoics in particular are engaged in the promotion of what might be called projects of justice. They exhibit compassion (if not passion) for others. And if that is true, doesn't it mean that subjective attraction need not involve caring and therefore suffering?

Let's assume for a moment that the invulnerabilist is right about this. Let's assume that it is possible to have subjective attraction without caring. (In doing so, we must keep in mind that in saying the invulnerabilist doesn't care, we don't mean she doesn't show compassion, but only that, in the end, the fortunes of the object of her compassion cannot matter to her.) Even if it were possible to have subjective attraction without caring, would most of us want it? Would we want to be the kind of people who are emotionally disconnected from the outcomes of our projects, the flourishing of those we're engaged with, or even the continued existence of those projects themselves? Would we want to be the kind of people who do not grieve at important losses? For most of us, sadness is not something we simply recognize or register; it is something we undergo. And if we make a mistake, an important mistake, if we do or fail to do something that leads to the suffering of someone close to us, do we not want to be someone who regrets it rather than simply noting that it was unfortunate and that we won't do it again the next time?

In saying this, I need to be clear. I am not saying that people want to grieve or feel regret. We don't. We would rather live without the emotional trauma that accompanies personal loss or failure, psychological distress, moral conflict, wondering about what might have been, or the fear of death. Even if we know that some experiences of adversity might make us better or stronger people, and even if, in the abstract, we would welcome those experiences, we probably don't want any particular one of them when they come along. It is not that we want to suffer but rather something else: each of us wants to be the *kind of person* who can suffer at certain misfortunes. Being able to suffer in the case of Large Matters is an expression not only of who we are but of who we want to be. I may not want those visits from the Queen of Darkness, to be sure, but if a close friend of mine is left by his wife or I neglected an important obligation to one of my children or my years of teaching turn out to have had no effect on students, I don't want to be the kind of person who shrugs and says, "Well, that's unfortunate."

Now the invulnerabilist might respond that wanting to be the kind of person who can suffer is just an unfortunate legacy that can be overcome. Perhaps it is just a cultural legacy, a way of expressing our compassion or, more broadly, our subjective engagement. Or perhaps not. Perhaps instead it is something deep inside of us, part of our human endowment. Nevertheless, through patient exercise, discipline, and training, we can be involved in the world in such a way that we need not suffer, that suffering will not concern us. We can not only get past the suffering but also get past wanting to be the kind of people who suffer.

Would we want this? Does it matter what the source or reason for our wanting to be the kind of people who suffer is? I suspect that most of us, even if it were pointed out that wanting to be the kind of person who can suffer in certain situations is a cultural legacy or at least an aspect of ourselves that we could conquer, would demur. We would not be attracted to a life without that facet of our being. This is because, for most of us, the capacity for suffering tied up with caring is bound to what gives meaning to our lives. Our lives are meaningful not simply because we participate in the projects we do, but because it matters to us how those projects and the people (or animals) with whom we share them fare. Otherwise put, even if it were the case that there could be subjective attraction without caring, that option would not allow our projects to confer meaning on our lives.

It is necessary to be clear here, because there is a confusion in the neighborhood. It is not *because* we want our lives to be meaningful that we care about our projects. Our projects are not simply a means to the end of having a meaningful life. Rather, things are the other way around: it is because we care about our projects that our lives become meaningful. We don't take up the projects, and particularly the central projects, that we do in the hope that they will confer meaning on our lives, that they will give us a sense of significance. That implies a too distant relationship between us and our projects. Instead, there are certain things we care about, things that matter to us to be and to do. And, as a result of being or doing these things, our lives take on a meaningfulness that they might otherwise lack.

It is often said that we cannot pursue happiness directly. Rather, it is in doing things we like to do that happiness arises as a byproduct. Of course we would prefer not to do things that make us unhappy. But that does not mean that we're pursuing happiness. What it means is that happiness and unhappiness serve as gauges for what we like and don't like to do. The same is true of meaning. We don't take up the projects we choose because they give our lives meaning. We take them up because we care about them, because it is important to us that they go well (and also, to be sure, that we want to be engaged in those projects rather than others). The meaning for us is not the cause of our engagement; it is the product of it.

None of this entails that we should not reflect on what makes our lives meaningful. We can, and many of us should, take stock of our lives, ask ourselves what makes them meaningful. In a previous book I argued that one way to think about what Wolf calls "objective attractiveness" is through what I call *narrative values*.[10] Roughly, the idea is this: There are certain themes that can characterize a life: intensity, loyalty, subtlety, spirituality, intellectual curiosity, and others. These themes can offer a way of thinking about what lends a life significance from an objective standpoint. They are ways of assessing life trajectories. If we agree that the appeal to narrative values (or some other form of assessment) makes sense, then I can ask of particular projects whether they will contribute to a narrative value that I would like to have characterize my life. Will this project lend intensity to my life, or will another one be better? Can I express my desire for spirituality better if I involve myself with a church or if I instead study the music of spiritually oriented composers?

It might seem at first glance that reflecting in this way would require that we choose projects based on their contribution to the meaningfulness of our lives rather than, as I have argued, the other way around. But it wouldn't. The relation between what we care about and our reflections on the meaningfulness of our lives is subtler than that. If we pick a project that we think will lend meaningfulness to our lives — lend it intensity, spirituality, subtlety, and so on — we must also care about the project in the first place. It must matter to us. A project that we did not already care about could not offer us the kind of nourishment necessary for meaningfulness. If I don't care about the importance or at least the worthiness of spiritually oriented music, then the fact that studying it might be a spiritual pursuit will not be enough for it to lend my life meaning.

One might object here by offering examples of people, say thrill seekers, who do what they do because it lends their lives intensity. Rock stars who are sustained by the intensity of live music scenes, rock climbers who seek the most dangerous routes up a mountain, ultramarathoners who want to push their bodies as far as they can go: aren't these examples of people who engage in projects not because they care about them but only because of the meaningfulness those activities offer? I believe the answer is no. The rock star isn't interested in doing just anything to get a thrill or lend intensity to her life. She wants to play music, just as the rock climber wants to challenge mountain faces. Doing these things matters to them. They usually seek to do them well, even if, for instance in the rock star's case, doing well might not mean playing music well but rather generating energy around her. Even if they would not do what they do if it did not offer them intensity, nevertheless the fact that they take up one project rather than another indicates their caring about that particular project. (To be sure, there are probably exceptions to this, just as invulnerabilists are exceptions to the idea of caring we have discussed here. But for most folks, caring about one's projects is not simply a matter of asking about the meaning they might confer on a life.)

To put the point in Wolf's terms, meaning arises not simply because of objective attractiveness but through the meeting of that attractiveness with subjective attraction. We must be "gripped, excited, interested, engaged" by what we are doing if our doing it is to confer meaning on our lives. And so asking which among the projects we might choose will confer that meaning is not divorced from—in fact it is rooted in—what we care about.

We have been assuming over the last few pages that the invulnerabilist is correct in thinking that we can have the kind of subjective attraction that confers meaning without it involving caring. I have argued here that even if that were true, most of us wouldn't want that kind of subjective attraction. However, we can challenge the assumption itself. It is not clear that, without caring, there could be anything like subjective attraction. The invulnerabilist secretes an emotional distance between herself and the world. This does not mean, as we have seen, that she cannot *act* compassionately. However, that act must be performed with a certain serenity, a certain distance from the world such that the outcome of the act cannot be of concern to her. One might say that she has a "preference" that the act have a successful outcome or that the people for the sake of whom she acts flourish; however, it is not clear what that preference amounts to (which is why I put it in scare quotes). She cannot be emotionally invested in the consequences of what she does, because that would require something like desire or passion.

If we are to capture the idea here, we might say that her act itself can be directed toward a successful outcome, but that the invulnerabilist cannot emotionally inhabit the act. Only in that way can she maintain both the compassion characteristic of several invulnerabilist doctrines and at the same time the serenity that lies at the center of invulnerabilism. But if this is right, then it seems difficult to say that an invulnerabilist can be "gripped, excited, interested, engaged" by what she is doing. She cannot be involved in it in those ways at all.

What we are describing here might appear to be a nearly inhuman way of living, and someone might wonder, as I do, whether anyone would really be capable of it. Although I don't want to deny that it is possible to live in accordance with invulnerabilism, it does seem to me to push the very limits of what humans can do. This might lead to the further wonder of why anyone would embrace any of these doctrines, if this is the counsel they offer. And certainly there are a lot of people who do embrace them. How can we explain that?

It seems to me that what people embrace when they think they are embracing various invulnerabilist views is something other than those views, at least in their official form. Instead, they are using the often valuable lessons of these views to live, not invulnerably, but rather *less* vulnerable than they other-wise would. Most Buddhists, Stoics, Taoists, Epicureans, and followers of Tolle probably do not want to rise above their de-sires or their passions but instead to be less in thrall to them, less bound to the emotional roller coaster that their wants subject them to. In this way, something very like invulnerabil-ism would be a welcome approach to Small Matters. In the face of train delays, overlong meetings, minor injuries, and other daily setbacks, mild disappointment at best is prob-ably the right reaction, rather than the anxiety and occasional anger that we are tempted to experience.

But what about Large Matters? If pure invulnerabilism is both a nearly impossible approach and, more important, not one that most of us would even want, is there anything that would capture how we might want to react in the face of de-bilitating physical injuries, tragedy to loved ones, moral con-flict, regrettable actions, and for many of us the prospect of our own death? Can there be anything resembling invulner-abilist teaching that might allow us to take some of the sting out of these events without requiring us to take the invulner-abilist path so many of us would refuse?

*

At this point let me return to a word we have invoked twice before: *acceptance.* We first considered acceptance in the pre-vious chapter, where it stood in contrast to affirmation. Con-trary to R. Jay Wallace's view, we need not affirm the unac-ceptable character of our past. We might value our existence and yet still recognize that it would be better if there had been a less barbaric past, among the results of which was that we did not come into existence. We might even prefer it. But we cannot do anything about it, and so we accept that we are the result of such barbarity. That acceptance is a more nuanced position than affirmation, which, as Wallace argues, leads to a "modest nihilism." It is instead a recognition of the tragic character of the past that led to us, a character we cannot change and need not affirm.

The second place we saw the idea of acceptance was earlier in this chapter in the discussion of Small Matters. There we recognized that what seem like Small Matters might not be so. There can be large effects of Small Matters that are beyond our ability to predict and therefore to take into account in deciding how we are to act or to react. We must accept the existence of unaccountable Large Matters that can result from Small Matters if we are to treat anything as a Small Matter.

What these examples of acceptance have in common is threefold. Two of these commonalities were suggested above in our discussion of the unpredictability of Small Matters, but it is time to bring each of them out more clearly. First, there is a recognition that some things are beyond our ability to control. We cannot control our past; we cannot mold it into something less grievous or deplorable. Nor can we control the unforeseen future effects of our actions. This is for the simple reason that we cannot foresee them. Another way to get at this idea would be to say that our history is contingent; it has no underlying order or meaning. This does not entail that everything is random or accidental, that there is no causality. Rather, the problem is that there are *too many* causal relations. Everything is a product of so many relations that it is impossible to grab hold of the meaning and flow of history and thereby to control it. I am the product, among other things, of the Holocaust, the

Magna Carta, the Black Plague, and Karl Marx's writings. The Small Matters that I try to keep in perspective might intersect with other Small Matters to produce Large Matters.

Second, those things that we cannot control may be important, and in particular they may be important in an unfortunate way. Of course they can be important in a fortunate way as well, a point we will return to briefly below. But, as sources of suffering, we recognize that what has happened and what can result from our actions (which we cannot predict) might have deleterious aspects, aspects that we would not ratify or endorse.

The third commonality is implicit in the first two. However, we have not yet discussed it. We act or react to these things we cannot control, not with serenity or affirmation, but with a sense that there is indeed what might be called a sadness to it all, a sadness to the fact that we are caught up in a web of history and events that outrun our ability to manage or regulate, a web in which we are inextricably involved but to one degree or another unable to discipline. (I use the term *sadness* here to gesture at something that is less despairing than resignation, less desperate than futility, less backward-looking than regret or remorse, and less intense than anguish.) We are the products of and actors in a world whose legacy includes us but outruns our will and the intent of our actions.

In the case of our being products of a tragic history, this sadness is evident. It is difficult to imagine anything other than sadness at the necessity of the Holocaust for my own existence. However, would we really say it is appropriate in the case of Small Matters possibly leading to Large Matters? After all, the unintended and unforeseen effects of our actions that we must lay aside in order to call something a Small Matter might just as easily be good ones as bad. The child that we produce because of our decision to eat in a Chinese restaurant during our adolescence might have a better effect on the world than the one we would have produced had we gone to an Indian restaurant instead. Why should we privilege unforeseen negative outcomes over positive ones if both are equally unforeseen?

To be sure, there is less sadness in the case of unforeseen effects of Small Matters than in that of our barbaric past. However, there is still a hint of sadness here. Most of us want to have good effects on the world. We want the world to be a better place for our having passed through it. To be told that in the end whether the world will be better off for my existence is something that cannot be foretold, regardless of my best efforts, is a saddening thought. It is a thought that, in order to call anything a Small Matter, must be laid aside. But it haunts my acts and, if I reflect on it, myself.

We might seek to be good people, and if intentions are all that matter, to the degree that we can control our intentions (an ability we raised doubts about in the first chapter), we might indeed be good people. But most of us want to be more than that. We want our actions to have contributed to improving the world. But this we cannot ultimately control, and therein lies the hint of sadness.

Contingency or lack of control in Large Matters brings a certain sadness: these are three elements of acceptance that characterize our previous examples. The third one implies a fourth, although they are so close that the fourth can be seen as an aspect of the third: this sadness arises from a *recognition* of the first two. We would not feel sad about our lack of control in Large Matters (not an utter lack of control, of course, but a certain lack of control stemming from the contingency of our history) if we did not recognize that lack of control for what it is. Instead of feeling sadness when Large Matters go wrong as a result of our actions we would feel simply frustrated or resentful or righteously unjust or even devastated—that is, if we even learn of them. It is the recognition and the quiet sadness that goes with it that either substitutes for these other reactions or stands alongside them, blunting their force. That is what makes it acceptance. Not affirmation, not serenity. Acceptance is something else, less peaceful than invulnerability and yet more peaceful than an abject subjection to the world's onslaughts or the modest nihilism that Wallace considers our proper relation to our past.

When the Queen of Darkness has her hand on my shoulder, or at least when I recognize it there, and I decide that, once again, I will soldier through until her visit is over, that is acceptance. When, in Susan Wolf's example that we considered in the first chapter, the mother faces the decision of whether to hide her son after he has committed a crime and, in deciding that she will, reaches a point where "the issue of moral approval" has "ceased to be decisive," that is also acceptance. When the promising athlete suffers a career-ending injury and then embarks on another career, always wondering whether she could have shone as a professional athlete but determined not to have that wondering dominate her life, that too is acceptance.

We can also see acceptance in regard to the vulnerabilities we discussed in the second chapter: the weight of the past and death. Several years ago I presented a paper on death to an audience of much older people. I argued that while death is a bad thing, immortality would be worse. The discussion afterward tended toward the relation these people had toward their own deaths, which for all of them were closer at hand than they would have preferred. The general sentiment was not Dylan Thomas's raging against the dying of the light but rather—and this is the word that most often came up—sadness. But that sadness was not resignation or depression. Rather it was an underlying sorrow that life would soon be over. Their sorrow did not preclude a gratitude for having lived, nor did it block them from living as fully as they could during the time that was still allotted to them. It was a sadness that stemmed from a recognition that death was something they could not control or evade and that it was going to happen to them, sooner rather than later.

The weight of the past, we recall, is the idea that none of us knows what another life arising from other choices would have been like. This tempers the regret or affirmation we might have in regard to the life we have chosen. Part of the weight is, as I have argued, normative. To the extent one is committed to the aspects of his life that give it meaning or happiness, he must also be committed to the idea that another life stemming from other choices might have given him more—although it also might have offered him less. It is at that juncture between what is and what might have been that we can see acceptance. The math teacher who did not choose to work for LGBT rights or study history but continued in her career (assuming that nothing happens to make her regret that choice) might accept both that other choices might have made life better and that she has no access to those choices because that is not how things work. Could there be a wondering, perhaps a wistfulness, about what else might have unfolded for her? Yes. But this does not mean that she need regret the life she has chosen nor wish for another one. She does not deny the weight of the past; she accepts it.

Here is another example. I am a New Yorker born and bred and have lived largely as a foreigner for the past two decades in suburban South Carolina. (New Yorkers, I suspect, rarely thrive for long periods outside their city, or at least some major city.) Sometimes I tell myself that my life is certainly far better here than most other lives on the planet. And this is certainly true. But this truth rarely seems helpful to me in those periods when I feel an exile. Instead, it more often leads to an attitude of "it's bad for almost everyone, except the lucky few." That hardly counts as wisdom and does little to comfort me. But suppose I think of it differently. Life is contingent. The very same trajectory that led me to South Carolina also gave me my family, my opportunity to study philosophy, many of the friends I have, etc., etc. Now it might be that a slightly different process would have led to a better life (in whatever sense of *better* one wants to use, which is itself a vexed issue). It also might have led to a much worse one. The fact is, here I am, with this life trajectory and these goods and ills, and there you have it.[11]

Like invulnerability, acceptance loosens the grip of the immediacy of our reactions or potential reactions to things we cannot control. However, acceptance only loosens the grip; it does not remove it. There is still pain and even suffering that comes from depression, the choice to leave morality behind, the injury that prevents an athletic career from unfolding, the recognition that another life may have been better, or the inescapability of death. With acceptance, serenity is not on offer—or at least it rarely is. This is because acceptance does not do away with passion or desire. It does not detach us from our emotional involvement in our projects. It does not secrete a distance, however small, between us and what happens to us. The world is always with us. Rather, acceptance allows us to recognize that relation for what it is and at the same time to recognize that the contingency of the world often does not allow us to accomplish what we seek in that relation.

Acceptance is the option we have if we choose to remain caring, as opposed to invulnerably compassionate, creatures. And the often muted sadness associated with it, along with the suffering that it does not preclude, are the prices we pay for the caring that we value. They are the other side of the subjective attraction that gives life meaning. Caring, we might say, is a package deal. Either we care and expose ourselves to suffering, or we are serenely compassionate and do not. And inasmuch as we want to be creatures who care—creatures for whom it matters how things go for the people and projects we're engaged with—then we cannot avoid exposing ourselves to the suffering that might, and usually does, attend to that caring. We can blunt the force of some of our suffering with acceptance, but we cannot occupy a space beyond it.

But if acceptance does blunt the force of our suffering, might it also blunt the force of our joy? After all, many of our joys are contingent as well. They arise from a set of circumstances that could have just as easily been otherwise. The easy child, the one who gets along with others and does well in school and isn't more of a pain during adolescence than she needs to be, is maybe a recessive gene or two away from being an inveterate troublemaker with periods of deep rage or depression. If her parents had procreated the night after they actually did, the latter child might have been born rather than the former one. They might well have loved the latter one, accepting that life is sometimes like this. But would acceptance play a role with the former one, loosening the grip of their joy with the recognition that it is just a matter of good fortune?

Acceptance doesn't play such a role, because it need not.

Good fortune is something we welcome, its contingency, if anything, enhancing our enjoyment. It is as though the universe has smiled on us, and our acceptance of its contingency does not diminish our joy. I am lucky that my offspring are well adjusted, and to the extent that I did not contribute to that state, that it is just a result of who they are, I am grateful. We accept our suffering—if indeed we do—because we must, because grief over a loved one or the end of a career or the failure to reach an important goal begs for some sort of solace. Acceptance provides that solace even where it does not shield us from its cause. Joy does not require solace; rather, it invites us to bask in it, the more so when it is unbidden.

This is not to say that all lucky joy is to be welcomed. There are joys we think we earn. When they turn out to be matters of luck or good fortune, it diminishes rather than enhances our pleasure. The person who gets a good job after an arduous set of interviews and tests will not have the joy in her accomplishment enhanced if she discovers that it was not the process that earned her the position but rather her supervisor's friendship with her uncle. The soccer player who scores a goal would not be happy to learn that, had the ball not glanced off the leg of an opposing player, it would not have gone in the net. On the other side of things, my pride in my accomplishments as a professor are—and should be—tempered by the recognition that I was offered opportunities for success that were never available to the person who cleans my office or the food server at the university cafeteria. This is not to say that I earned nothing worth taking satisfaction in. There are others in my position who have made little of their good fortune, as there are others who have made more. Rather, what is required here is to admit that my accomplishments are not all of my doing and that the person cleaning my office, had our upbringings been reversed, might now be sitting in my chair.

The joys that are undiminished by acceptance, then, are those that emerge from things that come to us unprompted by our own efforts. They are the pennies from heaven that periodically drop on those not plagued by persistent bad fortune. And because we do not need solace as a result of their appearance, our acceptance of their contingency does not diminish our joy. Rather, it allows us to feel that, for this or that moment, the wind is at our back.

Let us turn things over now and look at them from another side. If acceptance helps us loosen the grip of suffering but does not keep the world at bay, is it possible that there are experiences that are beyond acceptance, failures or losses or grief that we cannot or will not accept? Are there sufferings that overwhelm us to the point where we cannot—or we will not—diminish the anguish they cause us?

Let us recall the truck driver in Thomas Nagel's example that we considered in the first chapter. A truck driver fails to have his brakes checked. He is driving through a neighborhood when a child runs out from between two cars. Had his brakes been properly serviced, he would have been able to stop in time to keep from killing the child. Although partly his fault, his situation is also a product of luck. After all, how many of us have our brakes checked as often as we should? We can vary the example a bit to bring it even closer to home. Suppose, rather than a failure to have his brakes checked, he was going five miles per hour over the speed limit, which most of us do most of the time. Had the child not run out into the street—or better, had she run out into the street a little later, when, if he had been driving at the speed limit, he would have hit her—then he would have nothing to feel bad about. But that's not how things happened. She ran into the street, he did not stop in time, and now she is dead.

It is not clear that acceptance has a role to play here. It may be that, for the truck driver, his suffering is not to be abated by realizing the contingency of what happened, even less so by the contingency of the universe that led to his birth, her birth, and ultimately this moment. There are sufferings that, for those who undergo them, transcend the mitigation that acceptance might offer. The laceration the truck driver bears from this incident will likely remain with him for the rest of his life.

This is not to say either that acceptance will play no role for the truck driver or that it is unwarranted or inappropriate. Whether the truck driver accepts what happened is a matter of his psychological makeup. Maybe he does look at things from a cosmic perspective and can take comfort from the aspects of luck that helped create the situation. That depends on what he is like. The second issue—whether acceptance is warranted—is a trickier one. On the one hand, contingency did contribute to his killing the child, and it might not be unseemly for him to recognize this. On the other hand, that recognition can go too far, at least in the eyes of many of the rest of us. If, after the accident, the truck driver shrugged and said, "Yeah, I feel bad about it, but these things happen and it was just a fluke that she ran out there at that moment," we might feel that his acceptance was achieved at too low a price.

There are situations, then, in which acceptance does not play a role or perhaps ought not to. The latter concerns us less, since they are matters of ethics or morality, of the appropriate response to a horrible situation. In the case of the truck driver, what we want to imagine is that he cannot find a way to accept what happened. Whatever our moral or ethical reaction, we can understand this. His experience lies on the far side of the reach of acceptance. His exposure to suffering is beyond the consolations it might offer. Of course he would not be alone in this. There are people who will lose their own children; for many of them acceptance will be a long time coming, if it arrives at all. This does not mean that they cannot go on, that they will remain paralyzed for the remainder of their lives. Rather, it is that part of their existence will revolve around a wound that cannot scar over, much less heal. The contingency of the world, its extension beyond their causal reach, cannot serve as a consolation to them. They may spend the rest of their lives haunted by wondering what would have happened if they had kept their child home that day or had recognized the symptoms of the impending illness or had even just spent more time with her while she was alive.

It is not just the death of a child that can defy acceptance. It is easy to imagine von Stauffenberg, after his failed attempt to assassinate Hitler, sitting in his cell and refusing to accept that there are things one cannot control. More broadly, those who dedicate their lives to a failed project of social justice may find it difficult to accept that their context has thwarted their best and most considered efforts. Those who have sought a cure for a dread disease, followed the most promising clues, done the most diligent research, might not be able to accept the contingency of things when they find that they have been on the wrong path.

Beyond failures or perceived failures, there are other things that might resist acceptance. As we have seen, physical limitations, especially for athletes, can challenge it. Depression or other psychological afflictions can as well. For my own part, I can accept that the Queen of Darkness visits me, but that is only because I am lucky. My depressions do not plumb as far into the depths of despair as do those of others. I can hardly imagine the demons that grabbed hold of the wonderful writer David Foster Wallace in the years before he took his own life. And one can conceive, in the vein of the weight of the past, someone regretting her own life, knowing, just *knowing*, now that it is too late to retrace her steps, that she should have stayed with that man who wanted to be with her or studied poetry instead of psychology or moved out West with her friends when they asked her along with them.

Acceptance, then, has its limits, limits that are not just interior but exterior as well. That is to say, not only does acceptance not lead to complete serenity, it sometimes fails to alleviate suffering at all. It is a truce with the world that the world can sometimes break.

In this way, acceptance is irreconcilable with any form of invulnerabilism. For the latter there cannot be what might be called tragic situations, situations where there is no solace to be had. Because the world ultimately remains at an emotional distance, there is no suffering that cannot be eluded. To be overwhelmed by suffering is not to be regarded as misfortune but rather as failure. Tragedy is not to be recognized as a human possibility; it is to be overcome through patient exercise and discipline. As Rose Sayer, played by Katherine Hepburn, says to Humphrey Bogart's character in *The African Queen*, "Nature, Mr. Allnut, is what we were put on this earth to rise above." Acceptance, by contrast, because it does not prevent suffering, opens the possibility that there can at times be more suffering than can be dealt with, that suffering can be overwhelming. Letting the world in, refusing to keep it at a distance, means that ultimately we cannot control what might find its way in, try as we might. We can be touched by the world but also shattered by it. Creatures who can grieve in their vulnerability are also creatures who, at the limit, may find themselves folded into their grief.

At the beginning of this chapter, I said that vulnerabilism is not a project in the sense that invulnerabilism is but rather that it has some common themes. We can see those themes clearly now. If we were to create a credo that would sum up those themes, it could run something like this: Recognize the difference between Small Matters and Large Matters (or at least the provisional difference), try to quit suffering over Small Matters, and accept as best you can the contingency and uncontrollability of some of the Large Matters. Living in accordance with this credo could involve practices like those characteristic of invulnerabilism, such as focusing on the present and meditation, in regard to Small Matters. Taking account of the contingency of the world in regard to Large Matters might itself involve certain practices dedicated to helping gain perspective. However, where invulnerabilism has as its central project to instill serenity in the face of potential suffering through a series of exercises or practices, vulnerabilism involves different ways of coping with (and sometimes, as we have just seen, not coping with) the different types of suffering to which we may be exposed.

There are those who might read these reflections on acceptance and, while they identify with Buddhism or Taoism, Stoicism or Epicureanism or the writings of Eckhart Tolle, find themselves in agreement. I suspect, in fact, that most people will, to one extent or another. And they might say that their Buddhism or their Stoicism need not lead to invulnerabilism but rather to something like the acceptance I have outlined here. And with that, I agree. I am inclined to think that most folks who identify with one or another of the invulnerabilist doctrines do not actually seek the invulnerability that is their official form. They seek something less strict, something that can help them navigate the world without being unnecessarily buffeted by its winds but also without being rendered insensible to its storms. They seek something that I have described under the label of acceptance.

That, precisely, is the point of these pages. What people want is often not clearly recognized by the practices they undertake to get it. And because, as we saw in the first chapter, people are often molded by their practices, what they want is often not something that is clear to them. They are misled into thinking that their goal is something that it is not. If they had a chance to reflect on that goal and on the alternative I have presented here, they would choose the latter. But their practices are not structured to allow for making that choice, and so they remain unclear about what they really want.

The previous paragraph is written in the third person plural. It need not have been. It could have been written in the first person singular. As I stated in the preface, I have often been drawn to the doctrines I have ultimately rejected here, yet not without hesitation. These reflections are an attempt to understand that hesitation, to think more precisely about why I have always halted at the threshold of those doctrines. More important, though, they are an attempt to understand how it is that I, and I believe most of us, would like to relate to our own suffering, to our fragility. My hope is that many people will recognize themselves in these pages and particularly in this final chapter, that I am not alone in wanting to embrace acceptance and reject invulnerability. But of course knowing what we want is often, although admittedly not always, a better way to get it than not knowing, thus the need to work out the ways of our suffering, the limits of invulnerabilism, and the character of acceptance.

Philosophy has many roles to play. It has played many roles in my own life. Among philosophy's more important roles is to help us understand who we are and what we might want or should want. It is a role captured by the famous words of T. S. Eliot, "We shall not cease from exploration / And the end of all our exploring / Will be to arrive where we started / And know the place for the first time."[12] This is often difficult to do, and not always because we are distant from ourselves. Many times, it is because we are too close. We must see ourselves not from some outside vantage point but precisely from within the selves we seek to see. We ask who we are from the perspective of who we are, and we ask what we want from within the context of our current aspirations.

In thinking about our relation to our suffering, those aspirations have had as part of their context the invulnerabilist views we have discussed. If philosophy is to have an impact on how we think about our suffering, it must take up a critical relation to those views, asking about the truths that they offer and identifying the places where they fall short. And where they fall short, philosophy must, if it is not simply to be an exercise in demolishing idols, offer an alternative that at least does not fall as far short.

The alternative offered here, acceptance, does not render us immune to our suffering. It does not take us beyond our fragility. But neither does it leave us bereft. To accept the contingency of things and the quiet sadness that may go along with it is not to lie prostrate before the world. Rather, it is to embrace a perspective that can, with luck, help us find a path along the Large Matters through which we define the central aspects of our lives. It will not always do so. For some, those beggared by fortune, it might fail to do so. But if we are not, with Rose Sayer, simply to rise above our humanity, then coming to terms with the fraught nature of our existence is perhaps what is left to us, and acceptance is perhaps our means.

NOTES

CHAPTER ONE

1 Eckhart Tolle, *The Power of Now: A Guide to Spiritual Enlightenment* (Vancouver: Namaste, 1997), 33.

2 See, for instance, Bernard Williams, "Persons, Character, and Morality," in his book *Moral Luck: Philosophical Papers, 1973-1980* (Cambridge: Cambridge University Press, 1981).

3 Williams, "Persons, Character, and Morality," 12.

4 Todd May, *Our Practices, Our Selves* (University Park: Pennsylvania State University Press, 2001).

5 May, *Our Practices, Our Selves*, 8.

6 Jeff McMahan, *The Ethics of Killing: Problems at the Margins of Life* (Oxford: Oxford University Press, 2002), 229.

7 For more on Sharpe's life in football and then in prison, see Paul Rubin, "Waiting to Inhale," *Phoenix New Times*, June 6, 1996, http://www.phoenix newtimes.com/1996-06-06/news/waiting-to-inhale/full/, and Scott Bordow, "Luis Sharpe Looks Forward to Release and New Life," *Arizona Republic*, July 2, 1996, http://archive.azcentral.com/sports/cardinals/articles /2011/07/02/20110702arizona-cardinals-luis-sharpe.html.

8 *Luis Sharpe: Mountain Highs and Valley Lows*, dir. Brandon Garcia Madison Newman (KBM Productions), March 17, 2014, http://wn.com/luis_sharpe.

9 Susan Wolf, "Morality and Partiality," in her book *The Variety of Values: Essays on Morality, Meaning, and Love* (Oxford: Oxford University Press, 2015), 41.

10 Wolf, "Morality and Partiality," 44.

11 There is also an excellent discussion of the role luck plays in ancient Greek ethics presented by Martha Nussbaum in her book *The Fragility of Goodness: Luck and Ethics in Greek Tragedy and Philosophy* (Cambridge: Cambridge University Press, 1986). In particular, her discussion of Aristotle's thought in relation to luck has affinities with the perspective that will be developed here. We will see those affinities in the final chapter.

12 Thomas Nagel, "Moral Luck," in Gary Watson, *Free Will* (Oxford: Oxford University Press, 1982), 178.

13 Nagel, "Moral Luck," 175.

14 Nagel, "Moral Luck," 182.

15 Nagel, "Moral Luck," 179.

16 Nagel, "Moral Luck," 183.

17 Joel Feinberg, "Problematic Responsibility in Law and Morals," in his book *Doing and Deserving: Essays in the Theory of Responsibility* (Princeton: Princeton University Press, 1970), 34.

18 Feinberg, "Problematic Responsibility in Law and Morals," 35.

CHAPTER TWO

1 For more on narrative trajectories and their relation to well-being, see David Velleman's "Well-Being and Time," in his book *The Possibility of Practical Reason* (Oxford: Oxford University Press, 2000), pp. 56–84.

2 For more on coherence, see Antti Kauppinen's "Meaningfulness and Time," *Philosophy and Phenomenological Research* 84, no. 2 (March 2012), pp. 345–77.

3 L. A. Paul offers some similar reflections in arguing against the idea that one can make rational decisions about whether, for instance, to have a child. For her argument, see "What You Can't Expect When You're Expecting" *Res Philosophica* 92, no. 2 (April 2015), pp. 149–70, http://dx.doi.org/10.11612/resphil.2015.92.2.1. She expands her ideas in *Transformative Experiences* (Oxford: Oxford University Press, 2015).

4 The philosopher Galen Strawson has denied that his life is lived at all narratively in his article "Against Narrativity," *Ratio*, n.s. 17, no. 4 (December 2004). I discuss his view in the third chapter of my previous book, *A Significant Life* (Chicago: University of Chicago Press, 2015).

5 Derek Parfit, *Reasons and Persons* (Oxford: Oxford University Press, 1984), part 4.

6 Bernard Williams, "Moral Luck," in his book *Moral Luck: Philosophical Papers, 1973–1980* (Cambridge: Cambridge University Press, 1981), pp. 20–39.

7 Milan Kundera, *The Unbearable Lightness of Being*, trans. Michael Henry Heim (New York: Harper and Row, 1984), 5.

8 Kundera, *Unbearable Lightness of Being*, 5.

9 Plato, "Phaedo," in *Five Dialogues*, trans. G. M. A. Grube (Indianapolis: Hacket, 1981), at 64a, p. 100.

10 J. L. Borges, "The Immortal," in *Labyrinths* (New York: New Directions, 1962), 21.

11 Martha Nussbaum, *The Therapy of Desire* (Princeton, NJ: Princeton University Press, 1994), 229.

12 Borges, "The Immortal," 23.

13 I discuss this paradox at length in my book *Death* (Stocksfield, UK: Acumen, 2008).

CHAPTER THREE

1 Massimo Pigliucci, "How to Be a Stoic," *The Stone* (blog), *New York Times*, February 2, 2015, http://opinionator.blogs.nytimes.com/2015/02/02/how -to-be-a-stoic/?_r=0.

2 *Buddhist Scripture*, trans. Edward Conze (New York: Penguin, 1959), 56.

3 Theodore de Bary and Irene Bloom, comps., *Sources of the Chinese Tradition, Volume 1: From Earliest Times to 1600*, 2nd ed. (New York: Columbia University Press, 1999), 416.

4 Ibid.

5 Theodore de Bary, ed., *Sources of Indian Tradition* (New York: Columbia University Press, 1958), 101.

6 Ibid., 175.

7 Ibid., 118.

8 Ibid., 161–62.

9 *Buddhist Scripture*, 54.

10 Chuang Tzu, *Basic Writings*, trans. Burton Watson (New York: Columbia University Press, 1964), 36.

11 Lao Tzu, *Tao Te Ching*, trans. D. C. Lau (London: Penguin, 1963), 5.

12 Ibid., 46.

13 Chuang Tzu, *Basic Writings*, 117.

14 Ibid., 81.

15 Lao Tzu, *Tao Te Ching*, 6.

16 Chuang Tzu, *Basic Writings*, 39.

17 Ibid., 26.

18 Ibid., 60–61.

19 Ibid., 63.

20 Ibid., 32–33.

21 Ibid., 49.

22 Marcus Aurelius, *Meditations*, trans. Maxwell Staniforth (London: Penguin, 1964), 46. For an in-depth explanation of the rationality of the universe according to the Stoics, see John Cooper's excellent *Pursuits of Wisdom: Six Ways of Life in Ancient Philosophy from Socrates to Plotinus* (Princeton, NJ: Princeton University Press, 2012), esp. 157–84.

23 Epictetus, *Enchiridion*, trans. George Long (Mineola, NY: Dover, 2004), 1–2.

24 There is a complication here, one which arose in a conversational exchange I had with Amelie Rorty, from whom I learned much in my thinking about Stoicism. It might be impossible for someone to live a good life if he or she never learns what a good life is. Therefore, someone who is ignorant of Stoicism or has not learned its truths on his own might not have a path to a good life. However, that is not because the path is barred to him, but only because he has not learned of its existence.

25 Epictetus, *Enchiridion*, 4.

26 Aurelius, *Meditations*, 46.

27 Ibid., 45.

28 Ibid., 67.

29 Ibid., 48.

30 Ibid., 49.

31 Ibid., 83–84.

32 Epictetus, *Enchiridion*, 2.

33 Ibid., 185.

34 Epictetus, *Enchiridion*, 2.

35 Aurelius, *Meditations*, 147.

36 Ibid., 51.

37 Ibid., 85.

38 Seneca, *On Anger*, I.7.3.

39 Epictetus, *Enchiridion*, 12.

40 Epicurus, "The Vatican Collection of Epicurean Sayings," in *The Epicurus Reader: Selected Writings and Testimonia*, ed. and trans. Brad Inwood and L. P. Gerson (Indianapolis, IN: Hackett, 1994), 39.

41 Epicurus, "Letter to Menoeceus," in *Epicurus Reader*, 29–30.

42 Epicurus, "Vatican Collection," 37.

43 Ibid., 38.

44 Epicurus, "The Principal Doctrines," in *Epicurus Reader*, 34.

45 Lucretius, *On the Nature of Things*, trans. William Ellery Leonard, (Internet Classics Archive, http://classics.mit.edu/Carus/nature_things.html), bk. 2, Proem.

46 Epicurus, "Vatican Collection," 37.

47 Epicurus, "Letter to Menoeceus," 29.

48 Ibid.

49 Lucretius, *On the Nature of Things*, bk. 3.

50 Ibid.

51 The locus for contemporary discussion is Thomas Nagel's seminal essay "Death," in his collection *Mortal Questions* (Cambridge: Cambridge University Press, 1979), 1–10.

52 Epicurus, "Principal Doctrines," 34.

53 Aurelius, *Meditations*, 110–11.

54 Epicurus, "Letter to Menoeceus," 31.

55 Eckhart Tolle, *The Power of Now: A Guide to Spiritual Enlightenment* (Vancouver: Namaste Publishing and New World Library, 2004), 47.

56 Epicurus, "Letter to Menoeceus," 36.

57 Tolle, *Power of Now*, 49.

58 Ibid., 43.

59 Ibid., 146.

60 See, for instance, Charles Shaw's "Are You Unhappy? Is It Because of Consumer Addiction?" which has a number of references to other contemporary writings on the topic. Alternet, April 10, 2008, http://www.alternet.org/story/82013/are_you_unhappy_is_it_because_of_consumer_addiction/. Two other recent influential studies on the effect of consumerism are Juliet Schor's *Born to Buy: The Commercialized Child and the New Consumer Culture* (New York: Scribner, 2004) and Benjamin Barber's *Consumed: How Markets Corrupt Children, Infantilize Adults, and Swallow Citizens Whole* (New York: Norton, 2007).

61 Tolle, *Power of Now*, 63.

62 Ibid., 178–79.

63 Ibid., 223.

64 One of those exceptions—the only one of which I am aware—is the practice of narrative therapy, associated with the work of Michael White and
briefly referred to in the first chapter. By taking on theorists of injustice
such as Michel Foucault, narrative therapy has developed a more politically aware approach to its conversational work.

65 Adams, Robert, "Comment," in Susan Wolf, *Meaning in Life and Why It
Matters* (Princeton, NJ: Princeton University Press, 2010), 78.

66 An anonymous reader has called my attention to one bit of advice from
Seneca that seems to allow for grief. In "To Polybius," he writes, "Nature
requires from us some sorrow, while more than this is the result of vanity.
But never will I demand of you that you should not grieve at all." I read
this quote and the larger passage containing it less as a statement of Stoicism and more as a concession to the inability of most of us to live up to
its demands. However, even as stated, the idea of "some sorrow" seems to
ask of us to put more distance between ourselves and certain of our griefs
than should be asked of us, or than we would want to ask of ourselves. See
Seneca, "To Polybius" (Holy, Holy, Holy, http://thriceholy.net/Texts/Poly
bius.html). Earlier in this passage, Seneca states, "Do you lavish such upon
your brother, in such embalm his name. It will be better for you to immor-
talize him by your genius that will live forever than mourn for him with a
sorrow that is futile." That seems closer to traditional Stoic doctrine.

67 Cooper, *Pursuits of Wisdom*, 208.

68 For an excellent discussion of this point, see Chris Grau's "Love and History," *Southern Journal of Philosophy* 48, no. 3 (September 2010), 246–71.

CHAPTER FOUR

1 R. Jay Wallace, *The View from Here: On Affirmation, Attachment, and the
Limits of Regret* (Oxford: Oxford University Press, 2013), 257.

2 Ibid., 77.

3 Ibid., 187.

4 Ibid., 236–37.

5 Ibid., 238–39.

6 Ibid., 239.

7 See, for example, Craig Steven Wilder, *Ebony and Ivy: Race, Slavery, and*

the Troubled History of America's Universities (London: Bloomsbury Press, 2013).

8 Wallace, *View from Here*, 256–57.

9 As I was finishing this book, it was called to my attention that Peter Atterton offers similar reflections in his excellent short essay "Do I Have a Right to Be?" (*The Stone* [blog], *New York Times*, July 5, 2014, http://opinionator.blogs.nytimes.com/2014/07/05/do-i-have-the-right-to-be/#more-153516).

10 Fyodor Dostoyevsky, *The Brothers Karamazov*, trans. Constance Garnett (New York: Signet Classics, 1980), 226.

11 Shelly Kagan, *The Limits of Morality* (Oxford: Clarendon Press, 1989), 294.

12 Wallace, *View from Here*, 258–60.

CHAPTER FIVE

1 Pierre Hadot, "Spiritual Exercises," in *Philosophy as a Way of Life* (Hoboken, NJ: Wiley-Blackwell, 1995), 83.

2 Ibid., 102.

3 Tim Kreider, *We Learn Nothing: Essays and Cartoons* (New York: Free Press, 2012) 4.

4 Hadot, "Spiritual Exercises," 102.

5 Ibid., 108.

6 Susan Wolf, *Meaning in Life and Why It Matters* (Princeton, NJ: Princeton University Press, 2010), 9.

7 Ibid., 9–10.

8 There is a complication here. Subjective attractiveness might not always add to the meaningfulness of a life. If a person was really "gripped, excited, interested, engaged" in a project of evil, that might actually detract from the meaningfulness of her life. That is why I use the word *can* as a qualifier in this sentence.

9 Wolf, *Meaning in Life*, 4.

10 Todd May, *A Significant Life: Human Meaning in a Silent Universe* (Chicago: University of Chicago Press, 2015).

11 This paragraph is drawn from my column "Against Invulnerability," *The Stone* (blog), *New York Times*, December 27, 2014, http://opinionator.blogs.nytimes.com/2014/12/27/against-invulnerability/?_r=0.

12 T. S. Eliot, *Four Quartets* (New York: Harcourt, Brace, and World, 1971), 59.

SUGGESTED ADDITIONAL READINGS

Readings without citation here have their citations in the notes.

CHAPTER ONE

There are, of course, numerous writings on various types of physical and psychological vulnerabilities, both in fiction and nonfiction. There is also a vast literature in philosophy on moral conflict. I find Susan Wolf's "Morality and Partiality" to be one of the best discussions of the issue. However, Bernard Williams has a very different view of morality—that it should allow for partiality. See, for instance, "Persons, Character, and Morality." Martha Nussbaum's *The Fragility of Goodness* is a classic text discussing the vulnerability of morality to luck in ancient Greece. Regarding moral luck, where there is also a vast literature, Thomas Nagel's and Bernard Williams's articles of the same name are the standard starting points for contemporary discussion.

CHAPTER TWO

Although there are many treatments of issues like regret, I am not aware of any other discussions specifically of "the weight of the past" as I have articulated it here. The closest treatment

I know of is L. A. Paul's *Transformative Experiences*, which considers our ignorance of the effect of future experiences rather than the effect of past ones. On the issue of contingency and morality, the fourth part of Derek Parfit's *Reasons and Persons*, Bernard Williams's "Moral Luck" and now R. Jay Wallace's *The View from Here* are, to my mind, the best places to start. There are entire libraries of writings on death. My little book *Death* argues that, while death is bad, immortality would be as well. John Martin Fischer, among others, disagrees, arguing that immortality would not necessarily be a problem. See, for example, "Why Immortality Is Not So Bad," *International Journal of Philosophical Studies* 2 no. 2 (1993), 257–70. Among classic treatments of death are Tolstoy's *The Death of Ivan Ilyich* and, for the more philosophically intrepid, Martin Heidegger's chapter on death from *Being and Time*, trans. Joan Stambaugh (New York: SUNY Press, 2010), div. 2, chap. 1. Regarding life and narrativity, both David Velleman's article "Well-Being and Time" and Antti Kauppinen's "Meaningfulness and Time" are interesting discussions, as is Galen Strawson's delightfully provocative denial of his own life's narrativity in "Against Narrativity."

CHAPTER THREE

If I have used the terms "vast literature" and "entire libraries" to describe themes treated in the previous two chapters, I am not sure what word to employ regarding discussions of the philosophies considered in this chapter. My advice, for what it's worth, is to go straight to the cited readings themselves. They are usually readable, invariably articulate, and often profound.

CHAPTER FOUR

The starting point for further thought about the issues discussed here is, of course, Wallace's own book, *The View from Here*. Peter Atterton's short piece "Do We Have a Right to Be?" is a trenchant discussion of the contingency of our existence.

CHAPTER FIVE

Pierre Hadot's "Spiritual Exercises" is, to my mind, the locus classicus of discussions of the issue in ancient philosophy. Other essays in his volume *Philosophy as a Way of Life* would also be relevant. Recently, the philosopher John Cooper's *Pursuits of Wisdom: Six Ways of Life in Ancient Philosophy* (briefly cited in chapter 2) takes up Hadot's view of ancient philosophy as offering models for ways of living but emphasizes the role of reason more than that of spiritual exercises. For a more contemporary discussion, Tolle's *The Power of Now*, written in a popular vein, has much to offer. Regarding the meaningfulness of lives, Susan Wolf's *Meaning in Life and Why It Matters* is my favorite. My own contribution, *A Significant Life*, emerged from reflections on her book. For an overview of approaches to life's meaningfulness, Thaddeus Metz's contribution "The Meaning of Life" to the online *Stanford Encyclopedia of Philosophy* is an excellent place to start (http://plato.stanford.edu /entries/life-meaning/).

INDEX